how to be a grown-up

Daisy Buchanan

how to be a grown-up

Urano
publishing

Argentina - Chile - Colombia - Spain
USA - Mexico - Peru - Uruguay

© 2023 by Daisy Buchanan

© 2023 by Urano Publishing, an imprint of Urano World USA, Inc

8871 SW 129th Terrace Miami FL 33176 USA

Urano
publishing

Cover art and design by Sandra de Waard

Cover copyright © Urano Publishing, an imprint of Urano World USA, Inc

The first edition of this book was published in september 2023

ISBN: 978-1-953027-12-2

E-ISBN: 978-1-953027-16-0

Printed in Spain

Originally published June 26, 2018 by Headline Book Publishing

Headline Publishing Group Limited

Carmelite House

50 Victoria Embankment

London

EC4Y ODZ

Library of Cataloging-in-Publication Data

Buchanan, Daisy

1. Self-Help   2. Personal Development

how to be a grown up

Contents

For my sisters

Foreword

It was 4 a.m. on a dark December morning in 2014. All was calm, all was quiet. I might have been in New York, the city that never sleeps, but I was apartment sitting in the gentle Brooklyn borough of Park Slope, where everyone goes to bed by 8 p.m. because they have to be up with the sun in order to feed their babies. I'd been shocked awake by the sound and motion of my own pounding heart. As the sweat trickled and my skin prickled, I had my phone screen halfway to my face before I recognized that I was in the middle of a panic attack. After being diagnosed with an anxiety disorder in my mid-twenties, I'd accepted that panic attacks were part of my life—but it was the first time I'd been woken up by one. I was too sleepy to fully process what I was Googling at first. A few hours later, when I looked at the full list of my searches, I found "How to be thirty", "How to survive thirties", "Making the most of twenties", "How to grow up", "Am I grown up?", and "Am I enough?"

I couldn't quite find what I was looking for, so, eventually, when I'd calmed down, I decided that I wanted to write a book about it. I turned thirty in 2015, and while I didn't learn all the answers before my thirtieth birthday, I was able to start accepting that it was OK to still have lots of questions.

I'm a writer and journalist. When I was twenty-three I started work as a features intern on the teen magazine *Bliss*. I spent four years listening to readers and learning how to give them advice and support when it came to dealing with the biggest issues in their lives: friendships, relationships, ambitions, confidence, wellbeing, and how they felt about their bodies. When I left *Bliss* and became a freelance journalist, I was mainly writing for readers in their twenties and thirties, but I found I was covering the same subjects. The more I learned about readers' concerns, the more I realized that I shared them, and started to think that by writing about these subjects I could help myself and my friends, too. In 2015 I became *Grazia*'s agony aunt. Had I become wise enough to give everyone fabulous and life changing advice? Well, I wore spectacles in the profile picture, so I looked convincing. As more and more people wrote to *Grazia* to ask for help, it became clear to me that most of us already have many of the answers—we just need a big dollop of self-love and compassion in order to find the courage to do what we need to do.

I also realized that my personal level of life experience is the tiniest tip of the most enormous iceberg. Emotionally speaking, I'm Polly Pocket navigating the state of Texas. This is why I've brought a range of voices into the book—these are friends, and friends of friends, with compelling stories and wise perspectives on understanding the grown-up world. Most of them, like me, have an anecdote about a bad time, a sad time, or a moment in which something went desperately and horribly wrong, but turned out to be useful and life affirming. (Even if it was just in the sense that at the time, we thought the mistake might kill us, but then no one *actually* died.)

Most of us begin our twenties with similar hopes and expectations. Some of us are studying for degrees. Some of us have plans and ambitions and lists. Most of us don't have any money, or professional experience, or any real idea of exactly where the next ten years will take us. We might feel fearless. We might be frightened.

In my early twenties, I was a big, naive idiot. On the one hand, I'd sit through job interviews and ask about share options and pension schemes. I used phrases like "transferable skills" and prided myself on the fact that, when I was flat hunting, I'd always ask the landlord whether the property was prone to gas leaks—as if knowing that gas was dangerous was a hallmark of maturity.

On the other hand, I once took out a Warehouse store card in order to buy a scarlet sequined mini skirt that I wore for forty minutes before abandoning after realizing that I couldn't sit down in it without getting scratches on my thighs that made me look as though I'd been savaged by a weak, elderly tiger. One evening I got so drunk that I threw up in a taxi when I was five minutes from my house, and instead of heading home after I'd been booted out and fined fifty pounds, I walked in the opposite direction for ten minutes and got into a brand-new taxi. I once kissed a man who wore blue-tinted, wraparound Oakley sunglasses, indoors. I hid from my boss on a Sunday, when I was wearing my coat over my pajamas and buying onion rings in Tesco Metro. I truly believed people were interested in where I went to university, and that having a degree mattered more than being able to send a fax without starting a small electrical fire.

At the beginning, I was full of hope. I knew so little about the world and my place in it that I behaved like a puppy, so sure everyone was pleased to see me. I'd lick their faces, confident they'd make space for me on their laps.

By the time I turned twenty-five, I'd lost the naivety and was just a bit of an idiot. I told myself that everything bad that happened was OK because it was a "rite of passage". My bank cards being blocked was an early milestone, which would eventually lead to fiscal responsibility. No one finds the love of their life unless they go on a few dates with guys from Guardian Soulmates who order £80 bottles of wine, leave their wallets at home and then finger them in the park, right? Right? The harder I worked for almost no money, the more I was investing in my career. I was *supposed* to be permanently hungover, in the middle of a romantic disaster and jealous of everyone I knew! Milestones! Whoop!

But the more frenetic and "fun" my twenties became, the more I wanted a happy ending—and the harder I worried about not finding one. I even missed being delusional and over-confident at the start of the decade. At least I *had* confidence then, and some sense of who I was, however misguided. At twenty-six, I didn't feel any wiser or more accomplished than I had been at twenty-two. I just had a real sense of what my failings were, and a fear that life could only get worse. All that could happen was that I'd become more aware of how crap I was. I thought that as thirty drew nearer, success and happiness were supposed to float towards me like a drink on an inflatable coaster in the "Club Tropicana" video.

Instead, I was at sea, drifting away from the shoreline in the life-choice equivalent of a flimsy rubber dinghy. And every day, there seemed to be more sharks in the water.

Yet it did get better, in increments so tiny that they were impossible to measure. Quite by accident, by my thirtieth birthday I had fallen in love with a nice man and fallen into the career I wanted. But I felt so battle scarred that I couldn't let myself exhale. How could I know this wasn't a total fluke? When would I believe that everything would be OK?

I still don't. This book is partly about the realization that adulthood is in the eye of the beholder. No one really tells us how to grow up, let alone comes along and confers grown-up status upon us (although I still fantasize about a special maturity ceremony where I am awarded a big shiny medal that turns out to be a massive chocolate coin when you peel off the outside). Objectively, I know that I'm an adult, and I now have a husband, a healthy credit score, and a couple of nice handbags, and all the trappings that, if I were a lady in a book, would convince even the casual reader that I'm real—but I still worry that I'm really Tom Hanks in *Big*, and one day I'll wake up, brush my teeth, and see a child reflected back at me in the bathroom mirror.

Adulthood isn't a quest where you complete a series of tasks, acquire a collection of items, and are then granted the magical title. You can still live with your mum, or be an intern, or paint your nails electric blue, or go to sleep every night in a single bed clutching a cuddly flamingo, and be adulting. You're doing it. Every day you're moving a little bit closer to feeling it, too.

So, this book is for everyone who has ever woken up in the night and thought, "What am I doing, exactly? Is this it?", or just opened a Google browser and been tempted to type "HELP!!!!!!" It's for everyone who has ever thought about ending a date by climbing through a toilet window, or seen "insufficient funds" flash up on the ATM screen a week after payday, or gone to bed on a bare mattress because the soggy sheets are still stuck in the drier, and for everyone who has felt bewildered by the number of tasks they have to complete in order to be a basic, functioning human.

I'm probably not going to tell you anything you don't know, but I do want to say that the only difference between being a proper grown-up and an idiot sitting in her own vomit in the back of a taxi is perspective. You are not a goon among great minds. Every single one of us is a goon, hoping and praying that we don't get found out. And as you get older, you start to believe that just being is enough, and you don't have to wait to become perfect for your life to start.

All I have to offer is my mistakes. I had happy times and horrible times in my twenties, and much of it was of my own making, partly because of boys and booze and my bewildering fondness for embellished clothing—but mainly because it took me ages to realize that the only way to learn was by getting it wrong. I was desperately anxious about what other people thought of me, and whether I was going to get left behind, when I should have just worried about how much I was worrying. It has taken me a long time to realize that being happy doesn't have to be hard work, and if we endlessly pick at all of our past mistakes, we can never move beyond them.

We are our own harshest critics. If you ever worry about where your life is going, you're definitely moving in the right direction. You're capable of amazing things, but you might miss them if you don't stop comparing yourself with other people and their achievements. Don't worry about Instagram quotes superimposed over fake sunsets in which Marilyn Monroe and Albert Einstein are falsely credited with claiming that regrets are bad. Regrets are healthy, because they help you realize what you want. You can do anything within the realms of human possibility, because you're a human being. Getting enough sleep is much more important than having clean sheets. If you're brushing your teeth of your own accord, you're definitely a grown-up, no matter what you see in the mirror. Growing up is simply a matter of getting to know yourself, and accepting that if you think you're in the throes of a life crisis, the worst thing you can do is Google it.

CHAPTER ONE

How To Be Confident

The first time I ever felt consciously confident—properly, clear-eyes-full-hearts-can't-lose sure of my own efforts and abilities—I was ten years old and dressed as Eva Perón, aka Evita, the wife of infamous Argentinian dictator Juan Perón, and singing "Don't Cry For Me Argentina". (If you're not familiar with *Evita* the musical, it's a camp classic, and I'm a big fan of the mid-nineties movie version with Madonna in the title role, and Antonio Banderas at his most smoldering.)

It was in aid of a Brownie badge. At ten, I was a little bit old to be a Brownie, but my seniority worked to my advantage. In our troop, where I boosted the average age by almost two years, being able to tie your own shoelaces was an achievement. Just knowing all of the words to a song—any song—basically made you the Brownie version of Taylor Swift. As a small, rotund nerd with a talent that was entirely overshadowed by my own terrifying enthusiasm, Jester Badge day was an opportunity to demonstrate my love of the performing arts—in other words, it was a chance to be a show off. I knew the lyrics, I knew my audience and I was wearing the biggest, shiniest plastic clip-on earrings that a child's earlobes could bear.

One of the reasons that I remained a Brownie for so long was that the community center where we met on Mondays was the safest space I knew. (The first clue that I was not living my best life was that my happy place smelled of feet.) At school, I was bullied, mocked, and teased every day. At home, I was loved but tuned in to various family tensions. We were living in Buckinghamshire and my father was spending hours every day commuting to London, worrying about work and very aware that his wife and six children were entirely dependent on the income he was bringing in. My mother was spending almost every weekday alone in an isolated village with no one but six irritating infants for company. My sisters were small and stinky and constantly complaining when I stole their Skittles.

It was hard to find a corner of my life in which I could define myself before other people defined me. When I wore those brown culottes, I wasn't "Fat Fat Fatty" or "Sister Smelly Bum" or "Do-you-know-what-a-lesbian-is-'cos-if-you-don't-that- means-you-are-one! LESBIAN!" (In the early nineties, homophobia was more popular in the playground than Pogs, and Pogs were absolutely massive.)

So, as the other members of my Brownie troop and their long-suffering parents gathered to watch, I stepped out onto the "stage", a platform of heavy, grey-carpeted blocks that were usually pushed to the opposite sides of the hall for games of Red Rover. I smiled, graciously and gratingly, completely consumed by the fantasy that I was serenading my adoring people, not Mum and Dad and Mrs. Wills, who had been a little bit off with me ever since she gave me a lift back from Christmas fudge-making and I was sick in the cup holder of her Renault Espace. For the next four minutes, I sang, and I felt absolutely sure of myself and my place in the world. I knew I had nothing to lose, and because I knew everyone was going to be nice to me no matter what happened, I could revel in the pleasure of sheer showing off. My ten-year-old self, Daisy the Singing Brownie, is my confidence Patronus, and I've been trying to channel her ever since. At Brownies, I learned that, in some places, the world will take you at your own estimation.

In the outside world, I took my bullies at theirs. I was well into my teens before I worked out that no one punches you and calls you names unless they're terribly unhappy about their own lives. The bullies' work was so well executed, I looked for their calling cards everywhere. I went out of my way to search for meanness, because meanness was what I deserved.

Millions of us are bullied, and go on to bully others. It's a global, self-perpetuating evil, a little like an endlessly shared Hello Fresh subscription discount, or headlice. This is dreadful news when it comes to confidence.

It doesn't matter how clever, talented, beautiful, funny, fragrant, or good at card games you are. Without confidence, your skills will go to shit. They're not useful. Yet, you can go astonishingly far when all you have is confidence, and no other marketable talents. Please don't read this and go off to become a power-crazed narcissist, but do remember this—some people will find your confidence scary, and they will try to crush it because they are terrified of its power, but if you can hold tight, flex it like a muscle and make sure it's the first thing you think to fetch from the burning building, you can take over the world. You must use this knowledge for good.

I once interviewed a therapist who pointed out how strange it is that we accuse people of taking our confidence away when we're not born with it. Although it sounds tough, our job is to feed it, nurture it, and do whatever we need to in order to build it up.

My friend Frances is a jewelry maker. She started designing jewelry as a hobby but ended up turning it into a business. She says:

> *To be honest, I never thought about confidence that much, until I set up my own business. That was when self-doubt set in. I'd*

lie awake at night, thinking about every single criticism anyone had ever made of me. Who was I to quit a good, full-time job and do what I wanted? Did I have any right to believe that enough people would want what I had to sell?

Now I know that true confidence comes from surviving your mistakes as much as talking the talk. My business mentor has a very helpful theory about how our anxious natures are reasons to be confident. If we're inclined to think about all the reasons why we might fail, we're naturally good at risk assessment, which gives us a solid foundation for success!

I know that I have a lot to be proud of—I've won a few awards, I've been featured in magazines and I have some really stylish clients who love my work. But I'm prouder of dealing with disaster, such as when I lost a load of orders and the back-up file corrupted the computer, or having a cash-flow problem and persuading the bank to extend my overdraft. These were the worst things imaginable, but no one died. I didn't die. And no one came to my door to tell me it was all my fault because I was shit! It makes me think of surfing. Nothing can scare you once you've fallen off your board a few times and not drowned.

We all know that being confident is extra hard for women. It's like competing in a 200-meter sprint when you're the only one doing it as a three-legged race and your team-mate is a plastic beach chair that has been tied to your ankle. Every day, we hear this message: "Be the best you that you can be! But also, please be more like Michelle Obama, Taylor Swift, Beyoncé, the Pioneer Woman, and the latest winner of *Dancing With The Stars.*"

As a feminist, I think this is partly because the patriarchy is the biggest bully of all. We grow up trapped in a system in which men are expected to be endlessly confident without being expected to qualify it—but when you're a woman, your right to feel confident is constantly questioned.

To a frightened gentleman of a certain mindset and generation, the idea of self-assured women becoming powerful and stealing his eggs is more worrying than a *Jurassic Park*-style dinosaur uprising. This is why we are told to hate "chicks who think they're so great", how The Streets had a hit with "Fit But You Know It", why the most ardent Democrats are suspicious of Hillary Clinton and why everyone feels furiously vomitous when they think of Keira Knightley saying, "I look quite pretty, don't I?!" in *Love Actually*. For a long time, beauty has been the only confidence-boosting power that we have allowed and encouraged women to have, yet we're so angry and resentful when a woman wants to observe and own it that we become rageful about a fictional character saying it about her own wedding day.

The more I think about it, the more I suspect the Keira conundrum encapsulates our problem with beauty, confidence and women. We know she's gorgeous, so why is she fishing for compliments? If she's drawing from the confidence well, there will be nothing left for the rest of us but an empty bucket on a bit of string. I think this is the hardest confidence trick of them all. We must accept that an infinite amount of the stuff is available. Seeing other people being sure of their worth, or even looking for confirmation of their value, puts us on edge. It makes us feel as though our biggest frenemy just posted about buying four Coachella tickets and we can't even get on the site.

Throughout my twenties, my confidence flickered and flared. As I tried (and failed) to make bad relationships work, my confidence plummeted and I became convinced that I was a terrible girlfriend and no one would want me. We'd break up, and suddenly I'd feel as powerful as Zeus! Who cared about stupid boyfriends when I was so awesome and happy that I could probably manifest in different forms, and maybe even scare people by appearing in clouds? I worked at jobs where I lost all faith in my ability to turn a computer on, or find the toilets. Then, I'd leave, or get fired, and find myself more employable than ever before because I started to believe in myself again, and was spending more time doing what I loved and less time weeping over photocopier toner.

I'm glad that I've struggled with confidence, and that it's something I've had to fight for, not because it gives me a greater right to it, but because it makes me more aware of the boost it brings, and how important and effective it is. It also makes me wonder about the people around me. I lazily assume that a lucky minority of people are born confident, and have never experienced a day in which the world didn't work in their favor, but we don't know the specifics of how anyone came by their own confidence. If someone seems absolutely sure of themselves, their beliefs, and their brand, I'd be willing to bet that their confidence has been hard won, and they acquired it on their own.

The best thing about our twenties is that a steady confidence climb is pretty much inevitable. We begin the decade as a big ball of hope and ambition, with infinite ideas and almost no knowledge of how to put them into practice. We have a vision for our confident adult selves. We think that we'll spend the decade checking those boxes, measuring our confidence by our ability to sit at the head of the table in a board meeting, or get liquid eyeliner right the first time around without suffering from hand wobble and needing a spitty cotton bud. Now, I've discovered that the other key to confidence is perspective. It helps you to achieve and to meet the goals you set for yourself. It's also important to keep reassessing those goals, and to ditch them when they stop being relevant to your life.

Emma explains how her confidence was badly affected by goal setting, and she found it difficult to keep being positive about her abilities when she compared her life to her mum's:

My mum met my dad at university, they got married when they were twenty-five and she'd had me and my sister by the time she was my age. In my head, that was the goal—if I hadn't met the love of my life by my mid-twenties, and I hadn't, I should really worry. I'd failed. It was only talking to Mum about this the other day that made me realize how arbitrary this is. She told me she was a bit jealous. She wouldn't do anything differently, but in a different era she might have chosen to have children a bit later, and she thought I owed it to myself to change jobs, go traveling and experience as much as possible before I turn thirty-five! She also said that while she lucked out with Dad, most of the friends who married their university boyfriends are now divorced. She said that ultimately I'd draw more confidence from working to a timeline that was right for me than I would by achieving my ambitions at the "right" time.

Emma's mum is right—but it's very hard to see this when everyone around you seems to be meeting their goals according to a very conventional schedule. It doesn't really matter what you want to do, and plenty of people know they're not interested in taking a Game of Life route to adulthood, but I've always found it hard to stay in my lane, and not be distracted by other people's triumphs and achievements.

A couple of years ago, I spent quite some time sulking because Facebook told me that a clever, quiet girl with whom I'd gone to school had just qualified as an architect. I have made my peace with the fact that I don't enjoy math, or precision drawing, or any practical aspect of architecture beyond looking at nice buildings or wearing incredibly cool steel-framed glasses. But I felt winded by the fact that this girl had achieved something so impressive, and so measurable. This was the result of seven years of hard work. I'd chosen an entirely different working path, and one of the consequences of that choice was that my career goals weren't so clearly defined. There was no specific certificate or set of letters after my name that I could write a Facebook post about and underline with a row of party-hat emojis. I felt like a failure, because I didn't have anything that significant to define myself by.

My confidence was crushed because of the way I was choosing to value myself. At the time, I didn't really want to be an architect, or become a ski instructor, or have a baby, or buy a house in Hampshire. But, I was ready to feel defeated and less than myself because other people were meeting goals that I knew to be beyond my reach, regardless of my actual desires.

When I've struggled to maintain confidence levels, I've found it too easy to be lazy. If everyone else in the world is utterly bloody wonderful at everything, there's no point in me having a go. I may as well stay on the sofa wearing my questionable pink-toweling shorts, eating Double Stuffed Oreos.

This is why confidence is so crucial. It's petrol for your personality, and gives you a vital shot of positivity when you're feeling pathetic. It's the only reliable source of energy that can give you a boost when you're so uncertain of your place in the world that it's a struggle to dress yourself. So, how is it done? How can you think yourself confident in the time it takes to raise yourself from a lying to a sitting position?

Fashion editor and author of her own fabulousness, Diana Vreeland, often quoted Robert Louis Stevenson to her readers, advising: "The great affair is to move." She was talking about the nourishing, uplifting effect of international travel, but as long as mobility allows, the key to confidence lies in getting off your butt. The important bit is to get into your body before you get stuck in your head. I don't think life can present any problems that aren't slightly easier to deal with when you go out and get some fresh air.

Confidence comes with purpose, and as long as you're moving one foot in front of the other, literally or figuratively, you have purpose.

However, if you spend too much time trying to think your way out of a slump, you can end up stuck in a vicious circle. When I'm feeling low, I sometimes sabotage myself by making too many plans. I decide that I'll feel a bit better if I go to the gym—and drop off some dry cleaning on the way—and go back via the shops and pick up the ingredients for Beef Wellington—and make pastry—and while the pastry is chilling, download some software and start learning to podcast. But, I've got about eleven hours of downloaded podcasts I haven't even listened to yet, and everyone else seems to keep up with *This American Life*, probably while juicing and meditating, and why am I incapable of getting anything done!? What's wrong with me? And I'm back to sulking about my own uselessness before I've even got my sneakers on.

For me, confidence comes from achieving small goals, and it's easily derailed when I make a list of giant tasks that can't be achieved in a single day. So, I can cheer myself up and feel like a semi-successful adult by doing a load of laundry, or making a phone call that I've been putting off.

When I feel really low, sometimes I think of what people would say at my funeral. I'm not sure that any therapist would sign off on this, but there is no quicker, more dramatic way of comparing the way others see you with the way you see yourself. People have to be nice at your funeral, it's the law. No one is going to be at your graveside with a hanky saying, "She really was a sloppy drunk," or, "She would not shut up about wanting a dog. But she never got a dog!" We're unreliable narrators. We look at our own lives through unflattering filters. We get too close up to ourselves, and that perspective leads us to make the biggest messes—it's like seeing a barely visible spot through a magnifying mirror, leaping on it, and turning your chin into a pizza base. Essentially, we forget that we all have a lot to feel confident about, if you look at it the right way. No one else sees us failing in the way we think we are. They usually only notice the good bits.

The greatest confidence trick of all is that the whole concept of self-belief is a mad, farcical heist—a retro Hollywood comedy caper where everyone thinks that someone else has the suitcase filled with gold bars. We're all putting on unconvincing accents and chasing each other around in unstable vans, prepared to attack each other for the good stuff, when well-meaning friends placed the vital valise under our beds right at the start of the story. It's comforting to know that the most seemingly confident people have the odd wobble, and truly confident people, the ones who are really happy in themselves, don't need anyone to fail in order to be a success—they want confidence for all. Self-belief is a team effort, and a gift to be shared. If you love someone, give that person reasons to be confident in him or herself and the vibes will come back multiplied to you.

Confidence is the common factor here. It might get buried after a bad experience, but deep down, we know who we are and what we're about. Confidence will be there when the clouds part. However, we absorb so much uncertainty, negativity and fear that we—well, I—often worry that it's all been used up. My hypercritical inner voice is constantly saying, "You can't do that. Who do you think you are? Idiot. Get back on the sofa and return to the self-loathing." Confidence comes when you can get that voice to shut up.

DAISY DOES THIS!

➤ I think about what could go right. When I imagine the worst-case scenario, I think I'm preparing for the apocalypse and working out a strategy that will make me less vulnerable. However, I'm really just focusing on the negative, which is a confidence destroyer. To think about the good, positive outcomes of taking a risk makes me feel happier and stronger.

➤ If I'm feeling nervous and not confident about something, I spend five minutes doing something completely different, such as learning a new fact, or a word I don't know in a different language. To know that I'm slightly wiser than I was just 300 seconds ago makes me feel as though I have something to be confident about.

➤ I wear some proper perfume. My favorite is Penhaligon No.33, which is technically for men, but it has calming lavender, bergamot, and black pepper, and it makes me smell like a grown-up (or makes me feel as though a real adult is on the premises). Any fragrance you've worn during a particularly happy, ass-kicking time will help you hold your head a little higher.

CHAPTER TWO

How To Have Friends

Friendships can be the defining relationships of our twenties. It's the first decade in which we're allowed to choose the people we spend time with, and we work out who complements us and who reflects us as we discover who we are. Romantic relationships are in a state of constant flux, and even if you're lucky enough to get along with your family or have them in your life, they're under no obligation to be nice to you. The friends we make in our twenties are often the ones who see us as the adults we wish to be, which is great because they don't have any memories of the "sack-race incident" during sports day 1998, or any pictures of you that were taken after your mum cut your bangs.

A perfect friendship should be a long-lasting love affair. We should all seek to surround ourselves with people whom we choose, who choose us back, and make us feel ten times taller than we actually are. The ideal friend will cry with you, make you laugh until you're almost at the point of hospitalization, and filter your vision so that you see only potential and possibility.

If there is anyone out there who fits that description and has time on their hands, please call me.

As we become independent from the people who raised us, we hope to discover what the novelist Armistead Maupin describes as our "logical family" (rather than our biological family)—the friends who will love and nurture us thoughtfully and intensely, fix us when we feel like we've failed and sound genuinely delighted when we try to Facetime them at 4 a.m. because we "just fancied a chat".

However, I think that friendships are more like family relationships than we realize—there's going to be some bickering and resentment, the endless rehashing of old grievances and meals that end in surreptitious ankle kicking and pea flicking.

Over the course of your adult life you will find your tribe, but like falling in love, it might happen in a way that takes you by surprise. You will outgrow people, and they will outgrow you. As you get older, it does get harder to make new friends, but because you're wiser, your choices are better. If there's anything worth being fussy about, it's who your friends are.

I don't think I could have survived my twenties without friends by my side, but there were moments when friendships went wrong and made my life seem so bewilderingly hard and horrible that I started to wonder whether I'd accidentally become a contestant on a bizarre game show. I'd choose wrestling with a giant squid over verbally sparring with my pals. If something hurts in the playground, it stings like acid if you go through it when you're grown up enough to pay your rent and choose your own shoes.

When I left home and went to university, I discovered that grown-up friendship was harder than I'd hoped. I'd been very optimistic about higher education. I'd gone to an all-girls school and struggled to fall in with the right crowd—or any crowd, really—and I was excited about meeting people who didn't know my past, who hadn't nicknamed me "Hitler" because of the way I bent my hand from the elbow when raising it to ask a question, who had never seen me sing a medley of songs from *Les Misérables* while wrapped in my games towel because I'd mislaid the shawl that was a key part of my Parisienne crone costume. No one at university knew I wasn't cool!

I had a strategy for friend making. My plan involved buying and carrying a ludicrously expensive, four-inch long, pink Dior bag, a souvenir from my gap-year trip to New York, and drinking only vodka martinis (which was quite a shock once I found out what they really tasted like). Who wouldn't want to be my friend? I mean, I had proper highlights from a salon! These people had no idea about the years when I tried to do my own frosted tips.

Effectively, I turned up in character. I didn't really know who I was, so I went in Obnoxious Rich Girl Drag, and sure enough, I was sought out by an obnoxious rich girl! I was so relieved and overwhelmed that I had been chosen by someone that I just stopped short of offering to make her a friendship bracelet out of my own hair—a gesture that would definitely have blown my cover.

My new friend simply wasn't my kind of lady. Looking back, I suspect she was as insecure and nervous as I was, because well-adjusted people don't need to tell strangers where they went to school every five seconds. We attracted another gang member, a sweet girl from rural Scotland, who lived in our halls. Like me, she was trying to craft a new identity. She'd spent her school days in jeans and jumpers, feeling mousy and ignored, so by the middle of freshers' week she'd ordered some thigh-high pleather platform boots and had taken a delivery of a stripper pole. The first time we went out, she winked at a bouncer with so much pent-up sexual aggression that her contact lens fell out and we all spent the rest of the night searching for it on the pavement using the light of our phones.

The trouble was that I'd realized, too late, that I desperately wanted to be pals with the other girls in our corridor, and they, rightly, thought we were a bunch of losers. One of us was licking her thumb and rubbing her nipple at other people's boyfriends from home, another was tossing her hair and complaining about the lack of hot soccer players on campus, and the third (me) was constantly kvetching about the fact that she kept dropping her Dior in duck shit. We were not an attractive trio.

As I watched the others, and saw how their lives seemed to be led by passion and enthusiasm and a love of fun, not complaining, or treating other human beings like a Lovematic Barometer of Sexiness from a 1970s pub, I felt a bit sick.

How had I got things so wrong? There is no polite way of saying, "Sorry, I've had a think and I wish to cross over to the enemy camp because I don't like you." Also, how could I possibly convince the other girls that I was worth a punt, friend-wise?

Boringly, the whole thing came to a head over some washing-up, and a fight about someone eating someone else's pie. I tentatively made my feelings known—our lot was in the wrong, although I strongly suspected that a drunk boy had come in and raided our fridge. I discovered that the best way to make friends with the other girls was to shut up sometimes, listen and be interested, and stop showing off. I'm a lifelong lover of wanky bags, but good friends should be your mates in spite of the fact that you dropped too much money on the thing you keep your phone in, not because of it. Of course, I hadn't got it sorted by the end of my first term, but I'd made the first of many mistakes and learned that my mum was right. If you want to make the right sort of friends, the first and best thing to be is yourself.

Broadly, as it were, I've always found it easier to get on with girls. I went to secondary school with them. I lived with them, in a house that was 78 percent female—the only dudes were my dad and the cat. Admittedly, I've experienced bitchiness from women, and I've been a bitch, but I think the idea that women are meaner than men is a myth. When you give guys a chance to get their snark on, they really run with it. But I've always felt like a girls' girl, and found boys a bit frightening as a friendship prospect. Even when I started seeing my first boyfriend when I was fifteen, I did not do a good job of befriending his pals. I thought I was supposed to be distant, sexy and a bit haughty, once again ruining some great potential friendships because I was insecure and putting on an act.

Before I went to an all-girls' school, I was bullied by boys about my appearance, and the culture of the playground did nothing to promote good relations between the sexes. We thought of ourselves as cats and dogs (with the girls as cats, of course).

I ask my friend Ari, who teaches at a girls' school with a mixed-sex senior year class if she has any observations about gender and how school affects our later friendships:

I think that there are good and bad bits to the way our school does it. Your teens are so tough. Your body is changing, your mind is changing and you feel horribly self-conscious sometimes. I think that a lot of our girls find there's something nice about it being just girls, because it's one less thing to worry about. Their friendships are intense, and when things go wrong, devastating for everyone. Some other teachers take the "girls are naturally bitchy" line, but I think boys can be just as vicious, and perhaps aren't socialized to talk about the emotional impact of friendships in the way girls are. School is such a pressure cooker for those early relationships, no matter who you are or who you're friends with.

I'd say that at the beginning there is a lot of dressing up, hair tossing and excessive make-up application. And I think that most of the boys are terrified of these gorgeous, glamorous girls. But by the first half-term, everyone has got used to each other, they're back in hoodies and some very sweet, tentative new friendships start to spring up. In my experience, the gay students set the tone when it comes to mixed-sex friendships, possibly because life is so much easier when you can have a chat with someone who looks like they might make a good mate without worrying about whether you fancy them or they fancy you.

In a fit of misguided genius, I chose to live with that first boyfriend and his male chums at university, as we'd both ended up at the same one. I decided against an all-girl house share with my friends. The girls' house share went spectacularly wrong, and no one was talking to each other by the end of their first term together. Instead of losing my old friends to arguments about loud music and washing-up, I learned how to be friends with boys.

It's painful to admit, but if I'm honest I believed that the experience would have a sitcom quality. I'd sit around in tight sweaters, winning their unrequited love with a combination of breasts and delicious stews. I thought that, as the token woman, I was there to be fancied, and if I wasn't objectified by the boys, I'd totally failed. I came out of that house with a much better understanding of feminism than I'd had going in—a bit like being on *Celebrity Big Brother* with Germaine Greer.

Those boys treated me *as an equal*. They were interested in what I had to say, and would challenge me fearlessly if it didn't make any sense. They bought me pints in the pub and expected me to buy them back. When I broke up with my boyfriend and was incoherent with tears, they ordered me pizza and, not knowing what else to do, suggested that we all watch *Die Hard*. If they caught me wearing anything that suggested I had breasts, they would shriek and shout, "Bleach! I need bleach for my eyes!" They told me, in a matter-of-fact way, that when I had sex with my new boyfriend they wondered about ringing the RSP-CA because it sounded as though there was a baby seal cub in my room, and we were clubbing it to death.

I fell a little bit in love with one of them, obviously. He made it very clear that we were just friends, and that was all we'd ever have, but at the same time there was no "just" about it. He was the first person in my life to be consistently kind and uncritical, who made me feel cherished and adored while making it very clear that he wouldn't have sex with me if he was Indiana Jones and I was offering him all three Sankara stones in exchange for a quick shag. It was a valuable lesson, even if it took me an embarrassingly long time to learn it. Boys are not sex-crazed beasts from the Planet Willy. They are people, just like us, and they make brilliant friends.

I think the biggest benefit of befriending the opposite sex is discovering a brand-new perspective. You need friends who are similar to you, and friends who are different from you, and while shared interests and sensibilities aren't dictated by gender, it's important to become close to people who have grown up seeing the world in a different way from you.

We're told that the friends we make at this stage are the friends we'll have for life. However, we might feel as though we have become completely different people in our twenties from the ones we were in our teens. While we're out making new friends, what will happen with our old ones?

No one's life will stand still, and you might be the one who comes home at Christmas desperate to talk about old times, only to discover that your dearest childhood chums are moving to an ashram, or joining the National Rifle Association, or building a collection of semi-legal, poisonous snakes. You're all going to grow, and sadly that means that you might grow apart. What do you do when your friends don't feel like friends anymore, and is it possible to replace them?

I talked to Charlie, a Manchester graduate who says:

I cried on the day of my A-levels, because my best friend and I had both got the results we wanted, which meant we'd be at unis at the opposite end of the country. Three years later, when

we both graduated, we were barely in touch. We met up for a
drink at the pub we pretty much lived in throughout our teens,
and had nothing to say to each other. We hadn't fought, we'd
just become completely different people. I'd learned about con-
servation, become completely obsessed with traveling and was
planning a trip to Costa Rica. She'd fallen in love with a guy
who, to me, seemed like the most boring man on Earth. Our
friendship died. Nothing will ever bring it back. I have to accept
that we're both really happy now, and we were meant to be on
totally different paths. We've made an effort, and I was a brides-
maid at her wedding a couple of years ago. But, being with her
other bridesmaids, the girls who are her grown-up best mates, it
hit me that we didn't really have much of a foundation for our
friendship beyond flicking pen lids at our geography teacher.

Sometimes it's OK to let a friendship fall by the wayside, especially
if you mutually realize that your feelings have faded. Not all friends
are forever. Like Charlie, I struggled to stay in touch with most of my
old school friends, and it took me a long time to stop feeling guilty
about it.

It doesn't seem fair that, when we're students, and at our most un-
formed, self-conscious, and awkward, we have access to the biggest pile
of potential pals that we'll possibly encounter at any point in our lives.
But what can you do if you're socially stuck? To some extent, we're
expected to spend our twenties fending off endless invites and fretting
about our alcohol intake. However, many of us struggle with loneliness
and would love the chance to be a little more outgoing.

Finding a friend is like falling in love. To make it happen, you have
to be totally open to it, and find some joy in the fact that where there
are new people, you might be about to meet the One. Work is where a
huge number of grown-up friendships are built, and it often happens

gradually because you spend so much time with your colleagues that you're forced to find something in common with them. You might not adore your colleagues straight away, but they'll grow on you after a few months. If you start your twenties with a few friends, and put the work in, you can end the decade with a vast network, if that's what you want—because if each member of your core friendship group is meeting new people, those people might become your friends, too. We put a huge amount of pressure on our friendships, and we can define them in an extreme way. We think the best friends are the ones who say things like, "You could call me at 4 a.m. and ask me to come out and help you hide a body," but it's no good having pals who try to prove their worth with a clutch of (hopefully) impossible hypotheticals. The true value of a friendship group often comes from community, and feeling included. For the sake of your mental health, it's best to focus on finding friends who are *present*.

I met Charlotte at a party and was really moved by the story of what she did when a career decision affected her friendships and her happiness levels:

When I graduated, I was offered a great job with an energy company, which was based in Scotland. The offices themselves were quite remote, and lots of people worked from home throughout the week. I was the youngest member of staff by quite a few years, and the only one who didn't have major family commitments. After having a great social life as a student, the move was a total shock, and I didn't realize how hard it would be to live away from the people I knew, and with no real community to join.

I ended up deciding to find work in a different city. In a way, I appreciate what happened because it forced me to identify what I need. I realized that no job can really compensate for a lonely life, and I discovered that I can be confident and independent, but still need people around me—a social life is really important for my mental health. But I also learned that there are some benefits to being on your own, and I think I became stronger and more resourceful when it comes to enjoying my own company.

Moving isn't always an option, so it's important to think about how you can boost your social life if it feels less exciting than trying to watching paint dry. One practical piece of advice is to try going to one brand new place every week, and having a conversation with a stranger. It can be a coffee shop, a rummage sale, or a taxidermy class—all you have to do is find someone you like the look of, smile, say hello and try to find something out about them. They might become your new best friend, or, more likely, they might be your new friend's sister, or cousin, or hairdresser. All you can do is take a deep breath and see what happens, and if they're rude or weird, you never have to go back and do it again—just get on a bus and go to Owl Stuffing 101 in the next town.

Agata told me about how difficult it can be to make friends when you move to a brand-new country:

When I went to Spain to start setting up my business, I was all by myself, and it was miserable and terrifying. I sort of made friends by going to a class at a language school, and although it was definitely nice to have company, sometimes it made life feel even harder. We'd sit sipping coffee and saying things like, "Gosh, so hot today!" and, "That was an interesting class!" and I ached for people who understood me, that I could be silly with, where we didn't get stuck in a feedback loop of endless small talk. I had to get better at being on my own. I kept up the

coffees, and tried to see them as a social extension of the lessons
instead of an attempt to make brand new BFFs. I read a lot, and
went for long walks and visited galleries. It sounds so cheesy
and awful, but I guess I thought, "Right now, I need to be my
own best friend!" I tried to stop focusing on how alone I was,
and just had nice thoughts about how much fun it was to have
the freedom to explore on my own.

Eventually, spending time by myself paid off, because it
made me read a lot. I'd come in to a bar for a quiet drink, and
the bartender put down a copy of The Lacuna *by Barbara King-*
solver before serving me. Without thinking, I enthused, "I abso-
lutely LOVE that book!" and then thought, "Oh no, she's going
to think I'm a weirdo." But she was really excited to talk about
it with me, and that afternoon I had the best conversation I'd
had in months! She introduced me to some English-speaking
friends. We don't see each other much now, but we're all in
touch on Facebook. Honestly, it felt life-changing just to speak
to someone about something other than how hot it was. The
whole experience really taught me that you can't be mates with
everyone, so it's worth holding out for the good ones. And
sometimes the right new friend can pop up out of nowhere and
make your afternoon.

If we're dating online, why shouldn't we look for new friends online? Well, for internet dating to be successful it's imperative that you
feel smart and sane, and if you're socially isolated, you might not be
feeling like your best self—and there's a chance that you might miss a
few red flags, or giant, flashing, fluorescent banners. That's not to say it
can't work. It's just worth planning a strategy before you jump in.

Aneeta discovered this when she was a student on an exchange pro-
gram in New York:

It took me ages to make friends, and I felt like such a failure. I was in the middle of Manhattan, one of the most exciting cities in the world, people everywhere and no one I could talk to. In some ways I felt more isolated there than I did growing up in a really rural part of Devon.

I did my best to be proactive, but it wasn't easy. There was a Facebook page for the international students, and I thought, "I'll start posting, and arrange to meet people and that's how I'll make friends." But it was pretty grim. I messaged everyone with a polite, "Hello, I'm new. I'd really like to meet people. Let's get a coffee"—some ignored me, some assumed I fancied them and wanted a date, and some were just really, really boring, or rather, not right for me.

I'm sure their mates found them delightful, but there wasn't really a "friend spark".

I was on the brink of giving up hope when a miracle happened. I was getting coffee with a girl whom I'd already had one bad "date" with. I thought I ought to chill out and give her another chance. She brought an actual date—from Tinder—and bailed on both of us after fifteen minutes. I ended up having a really nice time with the Tinder guy—not romantic, just fun. We just found out we were both big fans of It's Always Sunny in Philadelphia, *I told him about how weird it was being an exchange student and he was lovely, and invited me to a party that night. We're still really close, and I ended up being friends with his group.*

That's a friendship fairytale for the ages. We can go through some lonely periods in our life, often when we're pursuing big goals and being really ambitious for ourselves. Being social can be hard, but it's never harder than when you feel totally alone.

The internet can be a great place for introverts to find each other. Maura, who works for a social housing organization, says:

To be honest, I'm not enormously sociable, and I really don't like going to clubs and bars. My people are the ones who like staying in, but we stay in together. Sometimes I think that it must be easy to meet new friends if you like big, mad hobbies. In fact, it's probably better if you don't like someone if you're going to shoot them with paintballs, or do civil war reenactments with them. But where are the social groups for the board-game players, the box-set watchers, the people who put their pajamas on the second they come home from work? It turns out that quite a lot of them are, like me, online and addicted to Facebook Scrabble. Some vague Facebook acquaintances have become proper friends thanks to Scrabble, and a few of us play together every day. It's a nice, no pressure way of building a relationship, and I love it because I don't have to be full-on, or worry about making a big impression. I think it's the friend version of having those awkward teenage chats with your mum or dad in the car, because everything feels less full-on when you're sat side by side listening to the radio. Sometimes chats happen organically, sometimes we play in companionable silence. I think it might be the millennial version of old men going on long, unsuccessful fishing trips.

If you too hate going out and don't feel like one of nature's Oliver Reeds, or even Tara Reids, there has never been a better time to make friends without leaving your house. I met about half of my grown-up friends on Twitter. Some are my ride-or-die, BFF, "Here, take my spare credit card and my kidney" pals. Some are gorgeous, funny people I like going for drinks with, and maybe three are people with whom I developed intense, internet friendships and then fell out horribly.

I still think Twitter is a brilliant place to make friends, but those friendships are forged in such an intense space that they don't always work offline. I've found myself having the sort of fights that seem so juvenile, you'd usually need a lunch lady to break them up.

The best, happiest examples of social-media friendship are my mates Lauren and Angela. I met Lauren because her little brother followed me and then tweeted us both to say, "Oi, Lauren, this girl sounds exactly like you." We were twin souls living in the same city, but our paths might never have crossed if her clever brother hadn't set us up. Even then, lots of tentative, friendly joke sharing and mutual internet friend harvesting was necessary before we plucked up the courage to say hello to each other at a big meet-up that had been arranged for female Twitter users. It was a brilliant event, and brought home to me that online friendships could have an even bigger impact on my life if I took them away from the screen.

I met Angela at a work party—we were writing for the same publication—but if it wasn't for the internet, I might have just said, "I really liked that woman", and never seen her again. Twitter allowed us to build our bond because we could chat whenever we were procrastinating on the internet, and that happened all the time. If we'd been relying on drinks parties and work events, I think it would have taken over twenty years to develop the relationship that we created in six months.

The internet is only as good as the people who are on it. If you are struggling to find people to connect with where you live or work, you'll probably find them online. Plenty of people aren't right for you, though, and you'll encounter those, too. It's just like dating, especially since it's easy to attract the wrong sort of people if you're not feeling confident, but if you're relaxed and don't take it too seriously, you'll have a lovely time.

New friend finding involves a lot of trial and error. It requires a real investment of time. If you were to think about it too hard, it would be tempting to give up and simply retire from civilization until your Netflix subscription expires. But, I promise that it's worth it, and if you focus your energy on being happy in your own skin, the right friends will find you.

Some of the friends you make in your twenties will be a part of your life forever. Some will stick around for a fun few months before moving to the other side of the world and you will forget to stick to Skype dates before growing slowly apart. Some will seem like the love of your platonic life, only to "borrow" your boyfriend and your favorite sneakers, failing to return either. It's OK. You don't have a limited window for making new friends. You're just learning the skills that you need in order to welcome the right new people into your life, throughout your life.

When it comes to people, you become fussier, and that's a good thing. Finding new friends as an adult is something to celebrate. Your first friends are made when you have no idea who you are or what you like. As you get older, friends are something that you can afford to get fussy about. When I was twenty-one, I was looking for the people who would help me to become who I am. At thirty-one, I am now that person, or at least fully formed enough to trust my friendship choices.

Can I "friend" you?
A guide to making mates online...

Don't start by approaching celebs—we'd all love to split a green juice with Cara Delevingne but she's probably got quite a lot on.

There's safety in numbers, so if you're friends with someone who's part of an intriguing group chat, join in, as long as you've got something interesting to say.

Have something to share. If it's interesting, funny or adorable, people will have opinions and the conversation will start.

It's tempting to rush into organizing a meeting if the chat is flowing, but hold your horses. It's a bit unnerving to swap a few jokes with someone and suddenly find that you've agreed to print off the two-for-one voucher for dinner with them at your local Chipotle.

Do not put all your pal eggs into the one-chum basket. Make friends with everyone at the same time. They won't get jealous of each other! Also, it will get easier the more you do it, and it would be a shame to waste all that lovely confidence.

Accept that most internet friendships are quite short-lived. You might end up spending your retirement holidaying together at Martha's Vineyard, but try to stay in the moment and enjoy every interaction instead of making big emotional investments in your potential pal.

... and offline

Be positive. If you give off fun, happy vibes, people will want to get to know you, and you'll draw them near, like a baker offering free, freshly baked brownies.

Offer people free, freshly baked brownies.

Be picky. It's better to hold out and wait for a great mate than it is to befriend the first potential pal you see. That's how people join cults and cross-stitch appreciation societies.

Behave like the sort of person you want to know. If you want a well-read friend, buy more books. If you want a friend who loves nature, get out of the house and see more trees. If you'd like a friend who knows about food, make a meal instead of ordering DoorDash—but find friends with whom you are already compatible. You might meet loads of new buddies at a carpentry class, but unless you want to spend part of your week up to your neck in sawdust, you might struggle to find common ground.

CHAPTER THREE

How To Survive At Work

Getting fired is probably one of the top five best things that ever happened to me.

I am honestly not sure that any human being has ever been as bad at anything as I was at my first job. I was sitcom awful. It was like being in a cartoon, with me loosening the anvil and then running under it in order to ensure that it fell on my own head. After the first month, I actually started to look for camera crews lurking in the stationery cupboard just in case it was all a big set-up, and someone was going to jump out and tell me what was going on when I'd lost the company's biggest account or made the coffee machine explode.

The role involved assisting the account directors at a small ("boutique") financial PR company. (Given that I once entered a room exclaiming, "My personal financial crisis is over! I just found Chloé sunglasses at 40 percent off!", I should have known I wasn't right for it before I applied.) But then, at twenty-two, I wasn't right for anything. I'd graduated two days before starting and was less well prepared for full-time employment than a newborn baby. Well, you can stick a baby in a pinstripe bib and they'll at least look like an old-school grumpy CEO.

When you finish your education, you're supposed to feel as though your whole life is ahead of you, the world is yours to explore and your potential seems like a brand-new jar of jam—you can't imagine ever running out. So why did I pick that job—and what went wrong for me?

Like most mistakes, it seemed like a good idea at the time.

I'd dreamed about spending my twenties working as a writer and living in London, and choosing a job in a slightly more stable, less exciting industry seemed like a sensible way of being able to tick two out of my three boxes. I left my student house on the Friday, and spent the next Saturday surrounded by boxes, trapped in a minivan on the freeway with a man I'd hired to drive me to my new London life.

I think that my main problem was insecurity, and I minored in impatience. I approached the workplace like I approached dating as a teen. I thought I'd be lucky to get anyone or anything, and I was happy to drop my professional pants for the first thing that came along.

Everyone asked me what I was going to do next, and getting a job meant that I had some kind of answer for them—not an answer I liked, but a full stop that I needed at a time when I was terrified of question marks.

The next eight months were the most miserable of my life.

I didn't really know anyone in London, although kind, well-meaning friends would come and stay for the weekend as, exhausted from a working week, I tried to stay awake for long enough to entertain them, while worrying about not having enough clean cutlery. I'd found my roommates on Facebook—Leeds graduates with whom I shared mutual friends. Naively, I assumed that we'd have plenty in common, and that they might include me in their lively social lives, but they only really became animated when they were complaining about local bus routes, and chose to engage me in conversation only when I was standing outside the bathroom, wrapped in a towel.

Once I'd paid my rent, bills, travel, and council tax, I had about £30 left over for the month. Then I'd get to work and my horrible boss would shout at me when his Gucci jacket fell off the coat stand. ('Pick up that jacket! It cost me £900, you know!')

I learned a lot, though. I discovered that owning a laptop and being able to write an essay on Gawain and the Green Knight in Microsoft Word does not mean that you have any meaningful or valuable technology skills. I was shocked to realize that presenting new ideas to your boss doesn't necessarily make that person happy and excited, because sometimes the harder you work, the harder the boss has to work, too. There's a time and a place for initiative and some people would rather you kept your head down, and did your best to keep the sobbing noise to a minimum in front of visiting clients. I also learned that I could be a real brat. Once I'd burned through my initial enthusiasm, I was naive enough to think that one of my colleagues would motivate me with kindness. But I was an inefficient human resource. London is packed with perfectly capable PAs. Once they'd learned that I was the most disorganized girl north of the river, they did not want me answering their phones and managing their diaries.

At twenty-two, I didn't want to be a square peg. I didn't realize that jobs are like relationships. You can't be right for everyone, and it's not fair to you or your employer to pretend that you can fit any mold when your passions lie in a particular area. I dreamed of a career where I could write, and pretended to myself that composing press releases allowed me to live out that fantasy. Saying, "I will look for a job at a magazine," made me sound like a grandiose idiot, even in my own head. I might as well have declared my intention to become the world's first giraffe psychic, or Rihanna. I was a resentful realist, perversely proud of my cynicism. Why shoot for the moon when you can go for low-flying light aircraft?

At thirty-one, I know that all the clichés are true. If there's a career out there that excites you, something you want badly, an idea or venture that is so precious to you that you can barely bring yourself to talk about it, only to get all weepy over it when you're a bit drunk, you have to try. It might not happen but attempting it will bring you so much joy, confidence, and self-knowledge that it will lead you to where you need to be. Doing what I did and deciding that you are not worthy of what you really want will only make you bitter, resentful, small, and sad. But your twenties are packed with false starts and mistakes. You do not know what you're made of until someone who smells of Drakkar Noir has reduced you to tears because you forgot to renew the Microsoft Office license.

My friend Amy also had a miserable time in her first "proper" job:

When I graduated, I worked with an awful boss on a start-up. He seemed wonderful at the time, a proper mentor, but as time went by, I realized he was a manipulative bully and the job wasn't what I'd been hired to do. He sapped my confidence, and I stayed there for two years. I wish I'd left after the first twelve months. I learned there's no point trying to give everything to someone who will keep taking from you, and that the people you work with should celebrate you and recognize your value.

Eventually, I was "let go". I was taken downstairs into a small, draughty room and given a break-up speech by my boss and his deputy—only they took great pains to stress that it really wasn't them, it was me. Even though I'd spent hours hiding in that room, drinking sour coffee, and pretending to be working while I sulked and fantasized about leaving, it was a horrible shock. I cried for about a week. I haunted London like a little ghost for two months, almost but not quite getting other gigs, until I moved back in with my parents in Dorset. I got a job at a call center in Bournemouth, where I spent 10 percent of my time helping people to renew their car insurance and 90 percent of my time apologizing to furious callers who did not want to renew their in-surance but had the money taken out by direct debit anyway. I'd come home miserable, dreaming about a fantasy life working in London and writing for a living, and comparing it with the reality of living at my mum and dad's and being shouted at for a living. To become a journal-ist had always been my big ambition, but then, growing up, I'd also wanted to be an actress, a ballerina, and an SNL cast member. Dream-ing was childish and, heartbreakingly, some part of me had resigned myself to the fact that grown-ups just didn't get what they wanted. Even though I'd been an enthusiastic student journalist at Leeds, I wasn't confident that I had the talent to keep going. My fellow hacks had been tenacious reporters, and I'd busied myself by making my assignments creative, penning a surreal music column and writing ridiculous bar and restaurant reviews, once covering KFC for a Valentine's Day special. Also, everyone else had been doing impressive work experience during the summer holidays, while I'd been working in my local supermarket, and unlike every other aspiring journo I knew, I didn't have a single auntie who wrote for the *Independent*.

I started applying for scraps of work experience only when I felt that I was hitting rock bottom. For a long time, I hadn't tried to get what I wanted because I was so scared of failing.

Then, I failed at the compromise job, and I felt like I was ready to take the risk. Obviously, I wasn't feeling confident, but at least being rejected couldn't make me feel any *worse*.

After three months of insurance by day and obsessive emailing by night, I received a message from the editor of *Bliss* asking me to come in for an interview for the role of features intern. I cried. I laughed. I was so overwhelmed and bewildered that I ran up and down the stairs, unable to sit still. I'd been so desperate to break into journalism that I'd applied for jobs to work for magazines about filing cabinets and ship-ping containers. *Bliss* was my hold my breath, shot in the dark, "This is *completely crazy* and it will never happen, but this job description could have been written by my guardian angel and I want it more badly than I wanted a tiny patent leather backpack after I saw *Clueless* for the first time" job. An editor of a cool, fun magazine liked my ideas enough to want to meet me. I had never been prouder or more scared in my life. "I won't get my hopes up, they'll be seeing loads of people", I told everyone, like a mantra, while murmuring, "But maybe... *maybe...*"

The interview wasn't the best—I fluffed a question on the Jonas Brothers, walked the wrong way out of the office and got so lost that I ended up having to phone a cab from a pub three miles away. So, I smiled about the "good experience", and set about sending my CV to *Crossword Compiler Fortnightly* and *You and Your Budgie*. Two days later, after fielding a complaint from a man who wanted to insure a car that appeared to be stolen, the editor of *Bliss* called asking me how soon I could start. It had taken me exactly a year since graduating, but I'd found my dream job.

Of course, it wasn't perfect. I earned even less money than before, fell into financial difficulties, and spent over three hours a day commuting, since the office was in the depths of Kent. At first, I was hired for three months, so I stayed with the boy I was dating in London "until I sorted myself out", which took almost a year and put far more strain on that relationship than it could bear.

But, the work itself filled me with joy. I had chemistry with my colleagues because we were all deeply passionate about what we were doing. My personality was an asset, not a liability.

Every day I had to come up with ideas, jokes, and creative ways of talking to pop stars. I was in my element. I would have paid to work there—when I think about what I was earning as an intern, I almost had.

I believe this is one of the most important things to learn in your twenties. Your talents will usually work best in a very specific space, and you need to try them out in a few different places in order to discover where they are most effective. It might be really hard. Ultimately, you might have to forge that space yourself, and build a home for your skills. The good news is that we live in a world that loves the self-starter. If you, too, dream of writing, but don't get to do it in your day job, you can blog or freelance. It will be very hard to start, and you'll have to persevere at times when it feels like there will never be any pay off, but it will bring you pride, joy, and confidence.

You can be passionate about food, fashion, sports, reading, drama—and create your own showcase for those passions. Equally, if doing what you love brings you enough joy on its own, don't be pressured to go pro. If you love cooking more than you love connecting with the world, you don't need to be a food vlogger—you can just focus on creating because that's the part that makes you happy.

Confidence is crucial here, but it can be hard to feel confident at work, partly because I don't think offices are designed, spiritually or practically, to nurture our best selves. Some people love the office set-up, but I've fallen in love with working from home. It's a place where I get to be the boss, but I'm not responsible for remembering anyone else's birthday cake.

Part of the problem is the structure of the working day.

We're supposed to spend eight hours in an office—seven if you take an hour for lunch, which you don't because that has been discouraged ever since they passed the law that forbids managers from calling their secretaries "Hot Lips" and chasing them around boardroom tables when everyone else was having a sandwich in the pub. We start early, we stay late, we stick to our screens, and still look at our emails when we're at home eating dinner. We're devaluing ourselves enormously, because we're at work or thinking about work every waking moment, which means our salary doesn't really cover what we're doing.

Many of us will give the company a panicky bonus hour or two at 3 a.m. when we can't sleep and start thinking about corporate strategy.

When you join an organization with this culture in your early twenties, you grow up believing that this is the only way to be, and quickly feel powerless, miserable, and out of control. If you can use mindfulness to challenge your negative thoughts and replace them with positive ones, you'll feel happier—and become much more successful, because that's how you'll be presenting yourself to your colleagues.

We all work very differently, and one of the most important things to discover in your twenties is that it's down to you to crack the code. You will realize that in certain conditions, at certain times, you are, productively speaking, hotter than sriracha on artisanal food-truck chili. You might come into your own at 8 a.m. or 8 p.m., but you'll know that no one can sustain hours and hours of work with no break.

The hard thing is that most companies will vaguely use expressions such as "flextime" and "bespoke working" while expecting to see a jacket on the back of your chair until after the sun has set. We've all had a boss who likes to sneer, "Leaving early, are we?" when you stand up at twenty to eight, having texted your mate to say that you're going to be late for dinner, and can he order you three big glasses of wine?

Laura, who works for a charity, hit on a genius solution—compressed hours:

> *I start early and finish late Monday to Thursday, which means that I can take Fridays off, because I've already got my work done. I was working ten-hour days anyway. We were offered the option because some working parents had requested it in order to spend more time with their families. I just feel like I've got a big slice of my life back! I had to spend years proving that I was valuable enough to the organization for them to recognize that they had to support the way I wanted to work. But increasingly, people in their twenties are asking for properly flexible hours, and slowly, new, young bosses are recognizing that no*

one wants to work until they fall over. We have to push, but it will get better.

So, when do we get to Level Laura? At what point do we become professional "enough" for our employers to want to keep us happy? Annoyingly, it takes time. We do need to prove ourselves, and show that no one else can do what we do as well as we do it, but we can strategically speed it up if we keep moving.

Annie, who works in advertising, explains:

I was delighted when I was offered a staff job at the company I had been interning for, but in some ways it felt as though nothing had changed. Everyone still saw me as the most junior person in the office. People who weren't in my new department would get me to do their admin. I was so determined to please them and show them that I could do a good job that I said yes to everything enthusiastically. After a few months I realized that I wasn't doing a good job for me. I'd spent so much time, and money, interning. I'd had to save up for ages in order to be able to work for free, but the situation I found myself in wasn't the one I'd worked for. It was like buying a coat on the internet and getting sent a cardigan—only I wasn't sure whether I was entitled to a refund. Eventually, I realized that the problem would only go away if I did. It took a while, but I found another job that was right for me, and going into a new place at a more senior level meant that I was perceived in the way I wanted to be. It wasn't about wanting a big title, or people running around after me, so much as actually having the time and space to do the job I had dreamed about doing for so long, without having to postpone it for long intervals while I did other people's expense reports.

Like Annie, I found that starting as an intern made it harder to get off the blocks. I thought I was doing my dream job, but as my twenties progressed, my dreams changed and the job stayed the same. After three years, I had a shiny new title, Senior Writer, but how senior was I really when I was being asked to climb into the recycling bin to retrieve a limited-edition doll of Oritsé Williams from boy band JLS? I applied for other jobs, and no one else wanted me. I begged for more money, and *Bliss* didn't have any.

My boss suggested that it was time for me to "spread my wings" and go freelance. She could give me almost enough work to cover my rent. I'd started to write unpaid pieces for other places, just to build up my confidence and portfolio, and was getting a tiny trickle of interest—not enough to pay a bill or buy my lunch, but the sort of commission that might cover a pair of socks on an instalment plan. It reminded me of the sensation I felt when *Bliss* first hired me—*someone* thinks I'm good enough! I'm allowed to be optimistic! It lit a pilot light of hope that kept me warm when I lay awake wondering whether I'd made a terrible mistake, and might have to go and live under a bridge.

A freelance career isn't right for everyone, but then I didn't think it would be right for me until I tried it. When I've been on staff, I've always felt like a nerdy, nervous child trying to earn praise from impossible-to-please parents. ("I was always disappointed that you never went to medical school. Why couldn't you have been a doctor?" "Um, this is a digital agency?") Liberating myself from having a boss by becoming one meant I wasn't vulnerable to infections from toxic work culture.

In all honesty, I think that I have three to four hours of hard work in me on any one day. I can do another two hours of busy work, emails and faffing about, and then I'm done. All my leftover energy goes into staying awake and possibly doing a round of Buzzfeed quizzes to help me work out which nineties sitcom character I'd most like to share a box of cereal with. Going freelance helped my confidence enormously because it gave me the chance to work on individual projects with a clearly defined finish line. I realized that if I spent the first part of the day writing, I didn't have to spend the afternoon stuck at my desk for the sake of it, feeling sleepy, grumpy, dopey and bashful because I was wasting company time. I was the company!

"I *love* freelancing!" I'd say to anyone who asked, and lots of people who didn't. "I don't think I'll ever work in an office again, if I can avoid it! They'd have to put the money on a flatbed truck and give me a crown to wear! Someone would have to offer me something spectacular!"

They did. There was one magazine that I'd wanted to write for since I was old enough to read things that weren't set at boarding school or written in rhyming couplets. In more fanciful teenage moments, I'd picture myself in a long leather coat, with highlights that had been put in by an actual hairdresser, a Chloé Paddington under my arm (it was the *It* bag of the Oughts embellished with so many buckles that you could use it to brain a burglar), at the offices of this publication, demanding champagne and murmuring about page layouts. One of the editors asked me to come in for an interview, and I presented my ideas with more untrained enthusiasm than a week-old spaniel. I'm not certain that I didn't try to hump her leg.

I was stunned when I was offered the job, and even more shocked when I had to leave after doing it for just three months. It affected my anxiety disorder so badly that I used to cry on the train home because I knew that it was only a matter of hours before I had to go back in again. The dream job was prestigious, grand, and glossy. I couldn't believe that the company wanted me. It was what I thought I'd spent my twenties working towards. I was prepared for any amount of hard work, and I thought that, after almost a decade of working, writing and earning, my foundations were rock solid, but the job triggered a personal emotional earthquake that shook me to my core.

Some colleagues were lovely, most were indifferent and one kept drawing me into a game that I really didn't want to play. She wasn't my superior, yet subtly, slowly, she'd put me down at meetings, shut down my attempts at friendliness and insert herself into projects I'd taken on in order to ensure they disappeared.

I thought I was going mad. I did go mad. She made me feel as insecure and useless as I did at twenty-two, but a glimmer of light and knowledge cut through my anxiety fog. I wasn't twenty-two any more. I'd proved myself in other places and I was big enough and ugly enough to cut my losses and get out. You could say that I let her win, but I think it's a little bit like the end of *The Little Mermaid*. I got my boyfriend to steer a giant, pointy ship into my nemesis and kill her! Well, not exactly. In the Disney movie, Ariel never wanted Ursula destroyed—she just knew that she had to get to a place of safety where Ursula no longer had power over her. Once Ursula lost power over all the people she intimidated, she had no more reason to be. So, I took myself away from the workplace and into a place of safety, and my former colleague no longer had the power to make me feel incapable or incompetent, because I couldn't let her into my headspace.

The idea of telling people that I'd left my fabulous, luxurious job was humiliating. No more celebrities, scented candles in the post or canteen privileges. I was worried that people would tell me I was a weak, crazy failure, but even my lowest moments were highs compared with the stress, depression, and anxiety I'd felt when I was there. Somewhere in the depths of my psyche, I knew that I had been brave and strong. Other people might have given both arms for the opportunity I'd just passed up, but I wasn't other people and I needed my arms in order to write. I'd just moved to get away from a person who made me doubt myself. I couldn't afford to let anyone else make me feel that way. It was down to me to define how successful I was, how confident I felt and how proud I could be of my work. It took me a decade to work it out, but it's a lesson that means more to me than any nomination, commission, or byline.

My friend Betty is, in my eyes, incredibly successful. She's one of the smartest and most ethically minded people I know. She has a senior role that enables her, literally, to make the world a better place as she's an environmental executive. But still, she can feel miserable:

I have too much to do, always. My manager says, "Don't worry about it. Just do what you can and if it isn't a priority, it won't get done, and it will probably sort itself out." He doesn't seem to understand how soul destroying it is to come home every night, or at the end of every week, and never feel as though I've had a good, productive day—because the list of stuff to do is longer than Harry Styles's public appearance schedule. However, I've come up with a solution. I still make "to do" lists, but now I end my working day by writing a "have done" list, and it helps me focus on everything I have achieved. I used to wake up in the night and start thinking of everything I had to do.

Obviously, it wasn't helpful. It just made me more anxious, stressed and scared. It hasn't stopped completely, but reframing the way I thought about my job has made a real difference. Now I'm approaching the list of doom in terms of tangible achievements, and I've started to feel capable again. My confidence is coming back.

I now make those "Betty lists", and feel stronger and saner for it. It also means that I approach each new task with a different attitude. Instead of thinking, "Oh, no! Another item on the endless list!" my brain tells me, "You can do this! You get things done!"

At twenty, you're surrounded by well-meaning people who want so much for you, but you might not know what you want. You might still not know by the time you're thirty, but you should aim to have a good idea of how different approaches, workplaces, and people make you feel. Your work shouldn't define you, but you should define the way you want it to make you feel. It's OK not to be ambitious in your career, as long as you're always ambitious for your own wellbeing and happiness.

Your career, and, most importantly, the way you feel about yourself within the workplace, is a little like climbing an infinite cliff face. The higher you go, the harder and steeper the path, and the more difficult it gets to breathe. You must make sure that you keep admiring the view and acknowledging how far you've come, if you want to keep going. There isn't a peak. If you're creative, or ambitious, or a bit of a perfectionist, you'll never reach the top—and the journey will never make you happy unless you learn to love the climb itself. If you don't, it's fine to come down and do something else.

DAISY DOES THIS!

➤ I make up silly, joyful passwords for any work-based accounts. I dread doing anything that involves an Excel spreadsheet, but I feel much more positive about the task and about work in general once I'm logged in as NinjaFirecracker007. (This isn't a password I actually use. Please don't try to hack me!)

➤ If I'm going to a meeting or a work event where I want to look professional, I worry about looking like me first and get bothered about the business element afterwards. If I turn up in a pinstriped jacket, I'll feel peculiar. If I arrive in a mustard yellow tuxedo blazer, I'll feel confident and kill it. As long as I'm free of soup stains and my secondary sexual organs are tucked away, it's all good.

➤ I always ask new contacts if they fancy a coffee, and try to meet at least one new person once a week. Sometimes it's good for me, sometimes I can help the person I'm meeting, but I think that hearing about the ideas and perspective of someone you haven't met before is always energizing—a work-out for your work brain.

CHAPTER FOUR

How To Be Social
(At Work And At Play)

When I was growing up, I believed that everyone was either an introvert or an extrovert, and of the two labels, "extrovert" was the one I thought I wanted to

write on myself, in neon pink highlighter, with ten exclamation marks. This is even though I was often consumed by a strong urge to hide behind a book and not talk to anyone, because speaking to anyone outside my immediate family made me feel cheek-flamingly self-conscious. But extroverts were fun, and successful! My parents told me that society had no room for people who would sooner burst into tears and wipe snot all over their cardigan sleeve than ask the bus driver how much it cost for a child's return ticket to Swanage.

I had to train myself out of it and work out how to be chatty and polite, even if I secretly believed that making eye contact with strangers might turn me to stone—as if they were all White Witches from Narnia.

I binged on old *Reader's Digest* articles with titles such as "Does Good Conversation Elude You?" and "Be More Popular at Parties!", basing my entire childlike persona on what was considered polite among middle-aged people in middle England. I learned that interesting people are interested people, that even grown-ups feel weird and awkward in social settings and that, usually, people at social gatherings are so scared of not having anyone to talk to that they'll be delighted if you introduce yourself and ask them how they're enjoying the fruit punch.

Now, I will say that Nathan from Year Six will not be impressed with your confidence and conversation if you walk up to him in the middle of "Boom! (Shake The Room)" at the school disco and say, in a trembling voice, "My, hasn't this weather been fine?" Generally, though, the *Reader's Digest* rules are pretty effective. Smile, be friendly, ask more than you tell, and hold on tight to the fact that everyone is as scared as you are.

Eventually, I tricked myself into believing that I was a proper extrovert. In a nice frock, with a large quantity of cheap alcohol in my system, I was very convincing. When I worked for *Bliss* magazine, I found myself at exciting parties with open bars three or four times a week. "I get paid to party! I am practically Paris Hilton!" I told myself. It was a topical reference at the time.

However, the reality of the situation started to dawn on me. Paris Hilton did not have to get up at 6.30 a.m. every day and spend over an hour on a train after drinking twice her body weight in warm white wine. Paris Hilton was also supposed to be spotted with her hair in her face, falling out of taxis—I'm sure this was mentioned specifically in her more lucrative endorsement deals. Paris Hilton was her own boss, and Paris Hilton would not get fired for throwing up on the boss.

It was a shock to discover that being social was not necessarily supposed to be fun, and that the people who had been professionally social for a few years now—the PRs and other journalists—were either terrifying cautionary tales who always seemed to be drinking off last night's hangover, or smart successful people who were not impressed by tipsy twenty-somethings who ignored their key messaging and just wanted to drain their booze budget.

I had a breakthrough when I was going out with my *Bliss* era boyfriend, who worked in banking. While I was out trying to win the title of "Drunkest person at the Sugababes album launch", he'd be at "networking drinks", hosted by lawyers, economists and various organizations who found it advantageous to have good relationships with people who managed money. (I'd like to think that this was just because they found math fascinating and needed a bit of help with the numbers round on *Countdown*.)

"Urghhh, these drinks are going to be awful, I don't want to go," he'd complain.

"But there might be little satay sticks!" I'd cry. "Plus you get free booze, and everyone will be a bit tipsy and you're going in order to chat to strangers. You might make fun new friends!"

He looked at me with a combination of pity and horror. "That's not how it works at all. All you do is swap business cards. Everyone is really boring. And the only people who get properly drunk are the handful of guys who are so senior that they could get their dicks out and wee into a wine glass, and it wouldn't hurt their career at all."

I started to realize that instead of being grateful for a job that let me go to lots of parties, I should start trying to be a bit more professional at the parties that I was going to.

White wine was my undoing. I didn't even like it that much, maintaining that a cheap red wine is usually drinkable, but white needed to be very well chilled and more than four pounds a bottle in order to be palatable. But white was what my colleagues liked, and for the sake of better bonding I followed their lead. If my brain was a computer that often overheated then froze on a sinister spreadsheet at the end of the day, necking a large glass of white wine was my mental version of pressing the power button for ten seconds in order to force a shutdown. I realized that I was not a naturally social person—I'd just socialize with anyone while I was drunk. Also, I was not that excited about meeting new people or spending time with old friends. I was just stacking hangover on top of hangover and trying not to think about the dull pain in my kidneys.

It took me a long time to admit that I'd mistaken heavy drinking for a social skill, and that I needed to work out a way of being relaxed, confident and animated that didn't depend on me working my way through my weekly unit allocation in an hour. While I should take full responsibility for my misguided enthusiasm for booze and the problems it can bring, I don't think it helps that I'm part of a nation of drinkers. So much of British culture centers around the pub, and I think many of us have become dependent on alcohol as a fast-acting, alchemic potion that transforms us from groups of grumpy strangers to gangs of glowing BFFs. And this is before you start thinking about the circular nature of boozing, which can take you on a 360-degree journey back to where you started and make you as angry and awkward as you were before you began. If you need an example, just get on any train in a big town on a Saturday afternoon immediately after a football match.

Still, when I think about after-work drinks, I'm filled with a cozy, creeping warmth. (No, not wetting myself—I'm not *that* relaxed.) A post-work pint is a form of communion.

Buying a round for people you work with is the only way we know to say, "I love you, even though I sometimes think about killing you." When you sit down with your colleagues at six o'clock, gin and tonic in hand and the weekend stretched out in front of you, as pliant and inviting as a very toned Pilates instructor, you're filled with calm joy. It's the holy grail of socializing. Network Valhalla.

But the pub of my imagination is so much nicer than the pub by the office. There's no bitching, the bathroom is clean, and there are no drunken smokers standing outside, holding cigarettes at hip level and flicking ash all over your favorite jacket. So I've been trying to work out how to harness all the best elements of after-work drinks—the bonding, the bridge building and the sense of closeness forged between people who have nothing in common but a hatred of the one broken office chair—without the wild, weepy hangovers, the rounds for people you don't really know but once signed a birthday card for and the risk of vomiting in the back of your team leader's hoodie.

Regrettably, the bad ingredient is alcohol. If you can work out how to have fun with your colleagues without strong liquor, you've got a trick to rival independent flight and invisibility. Booze is a false friend, and you can't make any valid claims about your brilliant social skills if, when you use them, you always end up waking up wearing your shoes and holding half a cheeseburger.

So, how do you bite your tongue and say, "Just a lime and soda for me, thanks!" when you don't know how you're going to make conversation with anyone for the next hour, and your body is screaming, "I'll have a pint! Of wine!"?

The first drink you don't drink is the hardest one to refuse.

Once you've sat down for twenty minutes and sipped a Diet Coke/ Virgin Mary, you start to realize that the ritual of drinking is as relaxing as the alcohol itself. It can be very hard to resist because, often, everyone around you will say, "Oh, no, go on! Lighten up! Have one!" which is daft. If you were cutting out shellfish because they made you poorly, they wouldn't say, "Just a little prawn cocktail, you've got nothing on tomorrow, it's the weekend—have the anaphylactic shock!"

My friend Lauren, a twenty-eight-year-old editor, is allergic to alcohol and sometimes becomes violently ill after just a couple of drinks. She tells me:

When I was at uni, I learned that I just couldn't process it—a glass of wine with dinner would make me feel horribly ill for a whole day afterwards. People would tell me it was just a hangover, and I'd think, "But I've seen people complaining about hangovers, and they get a bit slow and sleepy, and they're well enough to order Domino's. They're not taking to their beds for a full day afterwards, praying for death!"

When I started working in a big, social office, the pressure to drink was difficult to deal with. My line manager once suggested that I take a week of holiday in order to "build up my tolerance!" It was a really progressive, accommodating place in so many other ways, but when I didn't have a beer with everyone on a Friday afternoon, people would be giving me so much side eye that I'd wonder whether I'd accidentally farted without noticing.

After a little awkwardness—and some puking—I managed to stick to my guns, and proved to my line manager that it was possible to have a great, sober night out. I think it helps that I'm naturally quite outgoing, and I really made an effort to be social and go to activities and show everyone that I was still capable of having a nice time! Now, getting off booze for a bit has become quite fashionable, with Dry January and Sober October. People at work would get quite competitive about giving up alcohol for a month. I feel like I've been backing the losing team for years, and they've just hit a winning streak.

When everyone's on their second or third drink, and you're chatting, sober, and exceptionally well hydrated, you'll probably start to realize that it's possible to have fun, and easy conversations with colleagues and contacts, without being mildly tipsy. The temporary confidence that booze brings is replaced with a real, strong sense of self. You're a grown-up among grown-ups, socializing without the aid of vodka! You're a superhero!

I'm not advocating sobriety for everyone, or a return to the Prohibition era—partly because I don't think I could ever get my bathtub so clean that I could distil gin in it. Also, the best thing about having a night off when everyone else is on is that you often get cheerful and relaxed by osmosis, because everyone else is full of Bailey's and bonhomie. More importantly, you soon discover that you don't need to make a massive effort with drunk people. They're all repeating themselves, making spurious claims and slagging off the marketing department in a faintly libelous way, and all you need to do is nod and say, "Oh, really?" If you're a cunning bastard, you can work the loose lipped to your advantage—but more practically, when everyone else starts getting really boring at around 10 p.m. you can slip off without being noticed and go somewhere more fun.

If you're nervous, it might be better to be quiet and sober than tipsy and too friendly. For a long time, I made the mistake of forcing myself to be outgoing, because I believed that was the only way to meet people, even if certain big-group situations made me want to claw the walls and climb to the top of the nearest curtain pole like an actual scaredy cat. But you don't have to push yourself out of your comfort zone.

Consider Mr. Darcy. Do we care about what happens to the other, chattier, more gregarious men in attendance at the Meryton Ball? No. We're fascinated by the one who stands in the corner not talking to anyone.

To arrive at a party and start a conversation with someone you don't know very well can cause crippling levels of anxiety. It makes me think of jumping into an icy swimming pool and convincing yourself that if you move quickly enough, the water will warm up. However, there's no chance that a swimming pool will say, "It's been nice

talking to you, but I must go to the bathroom," and leave you standing alone in the literal and figurative deep end holding a small, soggy
bruschetta.

Marie, twenty-nine, a broadcast researcher and producer, says:

*I do a lot of freelance work, and while I usually get hired for a
new project because the person running it likes what I've done
in the past, it does help to go to industry events and network. I
used to be terrible at this. I put so much pressure on myself to
make an amazing impression on people, and I'd get so stressed
out that I never knew what to say. I'd either spend the night
hiding in the loos, or get so drunk that I'd wake up with no idea
of whom I'd spoken to or what we talked about. It never did as
much damage as I feared, but hungover paranoia doesn't do
anything for your confidence.*

*Everything changed when I met someone in the industry
who gave me great advice. I was supposed to be going to a
party with a director I'd worked with before, and ended up
blurting out all of my fears and telling her how scared I got
before events. She told me she used to be exactly the same, and
revealed that she got around it by changing her mindset and pretending to be a detective. Instead of going out and aiming to
impress people, she left the house with the aim of finding out
as many facts about the other guests as she possibly could. She
said that it was much harder to feel self-conscious when she
was asking people about themselves—because people love talking
about themselves.*

*And she would keep gently probing in order to find that
one strange, memorable fact—so the conversation would never
run dry.*

Marie's advice reminds me that if you're going to be social, it's important to remember your motives, and work out exactly why you've decided to leave the house. It might be to catch up with close friends, it might be to boost your career or it might be just because you think you'll have fun. Sometimes it's worth making an effort to go out and challenge yourself, even if you're feeling tired and grumpy. But if you can't think of a good, compelling reason to make the trip, it's OK to cancel as long as you're not letting down a lonely family member or messing up the numbers for a catered dinner. Our social energy isn't infinite, and it's much better to conserve it so that it can be channeled in an effective direction than it is to go to everything you're asked to, and feel burned out and weepy by Thursday lunchtime.

The other surprising truth that I discovered during my twenties is that, increasingly, there are times when I don't want to be around other people at all, and that's OK. A loud, sulky part of me wants to indulge in some teen rebellion ten years too late, to stop looking people in the eye and let myself turn into Ariel, the Antisocial Mermaid—because I wanna be where no people are. If you're going to socialize effectively, it's important to make time for some solitude and know that you can lock the doors and draw the curtains when you need to.

It's about negotiating your path as a person living in the world, and accepting that there will be times when you have to be social, even though you'd rather clean a toilet with your tongue, and in order to have the energy to deal with that, you need to conserve it.

Sarah, a thirty-one-year-old painter, says:

For me, the tipping point came when I discovered I couldn't go out two nights in a row. When I was twenty-one, I was out six nights a week. Then I reined it in a bit, midweek.

Then I discovered that it was taking me all day Saturday to recover from Friday, and I'd feel obliged to go out again because it was the weekend, and I'd spend Sunday thinking I was having a full-blown existential crisis. Heavy drinking and staying out late didn't help, but the part I really struggled with was having to be full-on. I'd go out in these huge groups, sometimes with people I didn't know very well, and I felt massively drained from talking to strangers all night. When I was with a small bunch of good, old friends, I came away feeling nourished and rested, but even the nicest new people made me feel a bit depleted.

I struggled because I still felt, really strongly, that I had based my personality on the fact that I loved meeting new people—that was part of who I was. And I was ashamed of myself because I wasn't enjoying my social life as much as I used to. I thought I was failing at life. Then I learned that most people aren't full introverts or full extroverts, and meeting new people uses a lot of energy—and it was OK if I only had enough energy to do it once a week, or a couple of times a month.

Like Sarah, I found that meeting new people became harder as I got older. Instead of rushing to house parties and embracing strangers, shouting, "Hello, friend I haven't met!" I became quite reluctant to stray from my pal comfort zone when I didn't absolutely have to. I'd see grumpy old men muttering into their pints of mild at my local, and instead of saying, "I hope that's never me!" I'd think "ZOMG! #Squad-Goals!" I learned that the more of a life you have, the harder it is to share it with people you don't know very well. When you're younger, and less fully formed, you can meet new people and make them into best friends based on nothing more substantial than the bands you like. Over the course of your twenties, as your life starts to align, your priorities shift. Your relationships become more rewarding, your work more challenging, and your sense of self becomes stronger. To some extent, we all believe in chance and fate, and wonder whether we're going to socialize with a mysterious stranger who might be the one to change our lives. Once we've reached the point where befriending strangers seems like a bit of an effort, it's usually a sign that we like our lives as they are. It's something to celebrate.

How to make small talk with a stranger

Dare yourself to speak to two people you don't know before you have your first drink. It will be horrible, and terrifying, and you might think you're going to be sick, but all you have to do is smile and swerve the salmon canapés. You'll feel like you've survived a scary social rollercoaster, but (hopefully) no one will have to go upside down.

When you're really nervous and can't think of an opener, try walking up to a woman you don't know and say, "I love your bag/shoes/hat!" People love compliments, and every accessory has a story. Maybe her mum bought it for her for Christmas and she hated it but lost the gift receipt and it sort of grew on her over time. Perhaps it was the last one in the Nordstrom sale and she had to fight off a stranger to get to it, using nothing but a Jonathan Adler cushion and her wits. Find the story.

Ask if she had far to come. It's dull, but people love to whine about traffic jams and rail replacement buses, and you can use boring journey chat to segue into where she lives, does she like it, how long has she been there, what sort of dogs does she see in her nearest park…

Don't overthink it. Small talk doesn't have to be witty, or scintillating, or scandalous. You can tell when someone thinks they are the most entertaining person in the room, because your internal monologue is saying "What a prick". Trust your instincts, which will definitely allow you to be fascinating and hilarious when the time is right. In the meantime, the person who has been talking about parking tickets for twenty minutes thinks you're the best thing that's ever happened to them, because you're paying attention to that big passion.

Keep the faith. You have a right to be in the room, and you're just as interesting as everyone else. You don't need to prove anything, or apologize for anything. Take some deep breaths and remember that grown-ups have to be polite to each other, and if anyone is rude, unkind or dismissive, that person has probably stayed out past their bedtime and shouldn't be engaged in conversation without the presence of a babysitter.

CHAPTER FIVE

How To Fall In (And Out Of) Love

In 2015, the love that dare not speak its name is the affection that a woman in her late twenties feels for her imaginary future husband or wife. The right person has to be out there somewhere, surely! As long as we keep putting ourselves out there, crossing our fingers, believing in fate, and avoiding cats and ladders, they must be coming for us! At twenty, we idly assume that we'll be married with kids by the time we're thirty. After we've turned twenty-five, we've set an arbitrary deadline with which to torment ourselves. It becomes less likely that we'll meet it with every year that passes.

Our mothers cluck, complain, and accuse us of fussiness.

We can't tell them that we're so unfussy that not one of our last three Tinder dates owned a set of bedsheets. We tell ourselves we're having fun. Another friend gets engaged and we mouth congratulations, roll our eyes, make cynical jokes about divorce with our other single friends, trying not to listen to the quiet steady voice inside us that's whispering, "Love is good. Fall in love with someone who loves you back."

At twenty-six, I seemed to be getting steadily worse at falling in love. Each relationship ended more traumatically than the one before it.

I'd approach each potential partner with a full heart, an open mind, and a clean head of hair, only to end up limping away with early onset PTSD.

I started the search when I was quite young. My parents still like to tease me about the day that I flounced down to the breakfast table in tears, wailing, "I'll be a spinster forever! I'll never even get to meet any men!" I was fourteen at the time.

But as the eldest of six girls and a student at a single-sex school, I grew up believing that my options were limited and I had to take what I could get. So, when I was allowed to go to a mixed Valentine's Ball the following year (it was in a local leisure center sports hall, and someone had stuck pink crepe paper hearts to the pommel horses), I approached the venue in the way a disorganized present buyer approaches a gas station shop at 8 p.m. on Christmas Eve. All the boys were shorter than I was, spotty, and tuxed up, apart from one who wore a blue shirt. I had my opener.

"I like your shirt!"

"I'm sorry, I can't hear you."

"I said, I LIKE YOUR SHIRT!"

"WHAT?"

We went outside and spent two hours talking about our upcoming history exams, and World War II. Then we dated for six years. After all, we had loads in common. We both thought Hitler was bad.

I had wanted a boyfriend badly—but I'd also wanted a mobile phone of my own, and a Saturday job. Anxious, nerdy, and not very confident, I truly believed that if someone—anyone—wanted to go out with me, I must be sort of OK. It honestly never occurred to me that I was enough on my own. I thought that nothing was as awful as being alone and feeling unwanted. Yet that relationship taught me that it's nicer to have no boyfriend than a bad boyfriend. It's always better to be alone than badly accompanied.

Looking back, every single friend and family member tried gently to remove me from the situation, encouraging me to stop seeking the attentions of a boy who constantly sulked, stamped and swore when he didn't get his own way. I was in love, but love had started to feel like the sensation of relief you experience when you stub your toe and it eventually stops throbbing. Eventually, I realized that drama doesn't sustain a relationship, especially when you're fundamentally incompatible. To be more honest, accurate, and cruel, I got home from a lecture at four o'clock in the afternoon to see my hairy, unwashed boyfriend playing video games in his hairy, unwashed bathrobe, and I thought, "I'm sleeping with that? Don't I have any self-respect?"

Aged twenty-one, I was single for the first time in my adult life. My friends were delighted, but warned me not to rush into anything, to learn how to enjoy my own company. I ignored them, and spent the next few months kissing anyone who offered. Surely it was better to get off with someone, anyone, than to go home on my own at the end of an evening, undesired? I was hot! I was discovering my sexuality! I was less subtle than a dildo on a drawing-room mantelpiece!

I had a short-lived fling with a sweet, funny boy named Dave, who accidentally fell in love with his housemate Hannah and dumped me after about three months. Ultimately, this turned out brilliantly, because after a further three months of misery on my side and awkwardness on hers, Hannah took me out for beers and bonding, and we're still the best of pals. Even dear old Dave is the only ex with whom I've managed to stay Facebook friends.

At the time, unsurprisingly, I reacted very badly to the dumping. I got back on my promiscuous path with a tenth of the joy and five times as much desperation as before. My confidence was shattered, and the pain the relationship caused me lasted for twice as long as the relationship itself. Then, just before I graduated, I met my banking boyfriend—the one I ended up living with for the first year of my time at *Bliss*. He was a grown-up with a proper job and a life, and I dazzled him. I was desperate to be the girl he thought I was. He thought I was perfect. If I could hide my flaws from him, maybe they would disappear forever.

It didn't work out. He was an economist with a binary brain and couldn't understand my fears and freak-outs. I was struggling with my sad PR job and then my thrilling journalism one, my identity and my new life in London. When I started at *Bliss*, I was always out or commuting, and although he offered to let me live with him, he became increasingly baffled and angry that he was working with millions of pounds every day, and yet had chosen to be with me, a girl who wasn't capable of making a hundred pounds a week. Also, I gained a lot of weight, and he was demonstrably cross about it. And he ruined a big family party because he wouldn't stop sulking about missing the Arsenal game.

When it ended, I was sad but philosophical. We'd tried our hardest, and we hadn't failed. We just weren't quite right together, like bits of brick that don't really tessellate. If you use enough cement, they'll hold a structure for a while, but it can't last. If you're not careful, everything will come crashing down, having lost its shape entirely.

With every ending, I thought I was getting closer to the beginning. Each violent tide would make me smoother, more rounded, ready for the Big Love that would make me into the woman I was supposed to become. When I fell for a very old friend, someone I'd known as a child, I thought I'd found it.

At first, I was very cautious. I knew that if the relationship went wrong, our friendship would suffer. After six perfect months, I dared to breathe out. That was when I learned that my friend was destructive, and desperately unhappy. He quietly hated himself and, by extension, the people who loved him.

Especially his own girlfriend.

He'd push me away as hard as he could and I'd come back, to "prove" my love. He could be so nice to me, when he wasn't being horrible. He told me that there was something wrong with me, and he'd drive me to therapy sessions as long as he didn't have to talk to me about my feelings. I saw a wonderful woman who helped me to see that I had long-term problems with anxiety, self-esteem, and self-worth, and who did everything but make a giant, light-up sign that said: "PLEASE LEAVE YOUR TERRIBLE BOYFRIEND". I stayed because he was supposed to be my happy ending, even though he made me so unhappy that I sometimes woke up crying in the night.

Eventually, he "ended" it, although there were another six months of break-up sex and weepy late-night phone calls. You could cut up a phone book with a plastic picnic fork more efficiently and effectively than the pair of us could finish that relationship. I went cold turkey, gave him up, and fell into the arms of an internet Lothario who was using his vague celebrity status to seduce every woman half his age in the south-east area.

I floated up out of my own body and watched myself getting thinner and sadder, dating dementedly—middle-aged divorcés, teenaged weed dealers, men who'd take me out and tell me about being in love with their colleagues and neighbors. All the while, everyone around me seemed to be making it work. I'd hear about a new engagement every week, and couldn't stop wondering whether I'd run out of time to meet someone and make a go of it. It was as if everyone else had passed Relationship Class with merit, and I'd failed the exam and the retake because I'd been failing to pay attention and reading Jackie Collins books under my desk. I felt as though I was at sea, and turning thirty was the point where I'd be unable to manage the current and find myself plummeting under waves.

Of course, loads of us do meet someone and make a good go of it before we're thirty. Often it works out. Sometimes it doesn't. My friend Rachel says:

I still feel so weird about getting divorced when I was thirty. I married my first proper boyfriend before I was ready, and it took me a really long time to stop feeling as though I'd failed. But we tried. We made a mistake, and millions of people make the same one. We grew apart, we couldn't agree on anything, and when we started talking about having children, we both realized that we didn't want to bring them into our sad marriage. Also, we weren't really having sex then, which didn't help.

At thirty-two, I'm starting to make sense of my single life. When we were planning our wedding, I was filled with a weird feeling that I couldn't articulate and can only understand now. We had a big, traditional event, and everyone around me was more excited for me than I was for myself. I thought that I was supposed to want marriage so badly, and I felt bad about being uncertain, so I lied to myself. I thought that if I told my head to shut up and went along with everything, I'd be happy. I met my ex when I was sixteen, and I thought that being miserable with him would be better than nothing. Being alone seemed unbearable. But even though divorce was difficult and painful, even though I moved out of our cozy flat and now I'm in a fairly grubby houseshare, and I've had to make new friends and rebuild life as I know it, I'm good. I'm better at being on my own than I ever dreamed I could be. I adore it. I love going for long walks by myself and choosing what to eat for dinner. Sure, I'm on my own, but I'm not lonely any more.

Rachel had to learn an important lesson about love in a difficult way. I think most of us need to hear her message over and over again. Marriage isn't an ending. It isn't the answer. To be happy, we don't necessarily need to be part of a pair.

Tia got married when she was twenty-eight. She says:

Among my friends, I think I was fairly typical—part of the first wave of weddings. It's been weird and wonderful. I love my husband so much, but the first year of marriage was hard. I thought it would make me feel grown-up and secure, but the adult nature of the situation and its permanence was a shock. Becoming a wife didn't change me, or give me any answers. I still had to find them for myself.

I wasn't the only one to struggle. I think I went to maybe eight weddings in that two-year period, and three couples are divorced now. It's so sad, but I think the real problem is that we're all told to believe in this happy ending without thinking it through, or asking ourselves if it's what we really want.

Several conversations I've had with my friends about marriage could have taken place in the eighteenth century. The smartest, sanest women I know have conversations about how and when their partners might propose, as if they are rare and temperamental pheasants whose boyfriends may or may not choose to present them with an engagement ring egg. We want to be chosen, we want to be loved and we don't know how to ask for this for ourselves.

Katherine, an editor, was gutted when her boyfriend didn't propose:

We got together when we were about twenty-two, and by the time my twenty-sixth birthday loomed on the horizon, people started to say massively unhelpful things like, "So, is Jeremy going to pop the question?" I became fixated, which distracted me from the things in our relationship that weren't working.

Eventually, when I was twenty-eight, he took me out to dinner and I thought, "This is it!" I dressed up, had a manicure in order to prepare for the ring selfie, ordered a glass of champagne—and got dumped! When I tell the story now, it makes me hysterical with laughter, but I was a wreck for a long time. Jeremy just got engaged to his new girlfriend, and I am emphatically single. A tiny bit of me is angry and sad that he didn't want to make a go of things with me, but that part is drowned out by the noisy sigh of relief that the rest of me is doing. I'm going to be single on my thirtieth birthday, and it's nothing to be ashamed of. It's a much better thing to celebrate than being married to the wrong person.

Some of us might look at our parents, or perhaps our grandparents, and envy the stability they found in their relationships, and wonder whether it was easier to build a life once you knew exactly who was going to be by your side. But perhaps in a few years, falling in love in your twenties and staying in love will seem as unusual and old fashioned as doing the same job for forty-five years and being given a retirement party and an antique clock for your mantelpiece. If that is your dream, I genuinely hope it comes true, but most of us will keep growing, changing and finding ourselves in different circumstances with every passing year.

In some ways, finding someone you want to be with forever and making it work has never seemed harder. In others, life has never felt more exciting. We're so connected that there's nothing to stop us from meeting people who live on the other side of the world, and if you make a mistake, you can call it a day and start again at any point. The main thing to remember is that no one *needs* a partner, and while your mum might go on at you about grandchildren, if you're single in this millennium, you're not going to be walked through the village and forced to endure a Parade of Shame. Remember, it's always better to be alone than badly accompanied.

DAISY DOES THIS!

➤ When I was single, or in a bad relationship, I could spend hours, days, and weeks comparing myself with happy couples and thinking about what was wrong with me. I worked through it by analyzing my envy and trying to discover exactly what was fueling it. It turned out that I was jealous of couples who liked the same comedy, ate delicious food together, and posted pictures in which they looked genuinely happy. It was a shock. I stopped fantasizing about billionaires who would whisk me off to Bali, and started to pay more attention to boys who put Seinfeld quotes on their online dating profiles.

➤ I tried to be patient with myself. My various break-ups made me feel deeply shitty, and it took me a while to work out that it was OK to mope, and I wasn't helping myself when my internal monologue went, "Stop moping, you silly cow! Get back down the roller disco!" Once I was dumped on a Wednesday, reactivated my internet dating profile on Thursday morning and lined up a date for Friday before I realized that it might be better for me to process what had happened before I nursed a flat gin and tonic and had a shouty conversation with a stranger who claimed to like "all types" of music.

➤ When I found myself on a bad date, I ran away. There is no greater thrill than realizing that if you don't warm to someone after the first half hour, there is nothing to be gained by giving them a second one for luck. I'd excuse myself, always apologizing but never explaining, and run home and straight into my nicest pajamas. Ben & Jerry's never tasted so sweet.

CHAPTER SIX

How To Love Your Body

The idea of loving your body is radical. As soon as you start digging your own flesh and bones, you're ready to start a personal revolution. It freaks people out. It causes commotion. But most importantly, it alters your own world view for the better. Learn to like the way you look as a way of applying an awesome emotional Instagram filter to your whole life.

A little while ago, I found a list of personal goals I had written when I was twenty-four, to be achieved by the time I was thirty. As well as "Become magazine editor!" and "Start pension!" I had written "Get dream body!" And I did it! I now have the figure of my dreams! My figure hasn't really changed much—if anything, I'm probably a bit fatter. I just worked out the difference between my own fantasy and the one that actually belonged to advertisers and magazines.

When I was growing up, I had no idea that loving my body without changing it was an option. I was tall and heavy, quiet and clever. I was usually top of the class, and I would have given up half of my brain power just to be a couple of pounds lighter. Occasionally, someone would say something kind like, "You could be almost pretty, if you weren't quite so overweight." The last word was whispered, as though the size of my body was a shameful secret.

That was when the school bullies weren't physically and verbally abusing me, sometimes kicking me in the face and demanding my lunch, while claiming that by depriving me of food they were doing me a favor.

I joke about it now—"I was such a poindexter! I would have kicked me in the face, too!"—but being bullied about my body was horrible! My parents got so angry on my behalf that it was easier to stop telling them about it. I believed I had no more control over the bullying than I did over weather patterns and TV schedules. Also, as the eldest daughter of a big Catholic family, I found it hard to tell my family how I felt, and why I cared. My parents wanted their kids clean and covered up. It was easier to tell me that the way I looked didn't matter at all—God just wanted me to do well at school, set a good example for my sisters and not commit the sin of vanity. For a while, becoming a saint seemed like a sensible career choice for me. They were often hideously disfigured, and famously "pure". No one would ever want to have sex with me anyway, so I just had to endure the beatings silently until I got canonized. It was a great plan!

Then I went to my smart all-girls' secondary school, and some of my wish came true. I did lose half of my brain power! Suddenly, I was surrounded by exceptionally clever, slender girls. Being smart had been part of my identity, and I wasn't the smartest anymore. Even though I was just as intelligent as I had always been, I *felt* stupid. I was out of my depth. I was also startled by puberty. I still had the face of a child, but suddenly I owned a tiny waist and the tits of a glamour model. Strange men started to notice me in a way that made me miss the beatings. I still felt grotesque. I'd grown up dealing with people making unsolicited comments about my body, and I was constantly, horribly self-conscious. So, I tried to disappear.

I was not the only one. Stick almost any group of academically in-clined adolescent girls together, and some of them will have more food issues than you could find at *Good Housekeeping* HQ. My plump best friend became scarily skinny as she worked out how to deal with her parents' break-up. She was full of tips and tricks, and soon I followed suit. Constant hunger made me feel powerful, for the first time. I was in charge of my body, and I could master my own greed.

Occasionally, I'd slip up, and I spent a couple of tearful Boxing Days regurgitating turkey sandwiches. At first, my self-control was praised, as I'd stopped misery eating third helpings of pudding. My grades shot up, too, because I was spending lunchtimes hiding in the library. I set myself high standards, and I could only begin to accept myself if I achieved straight As and A*s, and stayed under 300 calories a day.

When everyone started audibly worrying about how thin I was, I started to dress in extra layers. It didn't matter whether I was fat or thin, everyone felt entitled to comment on my body in a way that sug-gested their opinions were more important than the way I felt. It sucked.

Anorexia is all consuming. Luckily, I reached a point where I had to choose between fun and calorie counting, and I chose fun. After going to that dance with my arsenal of awkward shirt compliments, I suddenly found myself with a real-life boyfriend. The joy and excite-ment that generated gave me the tools to build the ladder I needed to open the window and climb out of my own head. I made friends who celebrated my nerdiness. They wanted to know about the music I loved and the books I read, not how I hadn't eaten ice cream since February 1999. Slowly, so slowly, the beat of my body changed, and as soon as I stopped trying to control its rhythm I could dance to it. As I will explain later, literally getting in touch with my body was one of the activities that helped the most. My dormant hormones woke up and I took to masturbation with alacrity and enthusiasm. Who cares about being able to zip up size zero jeans when they can make themselves come!?

As someone who has recovered from an eating disorder, I find that food issues are a bit like herpes. They never truly go away, they're infectious, and if you scratch them too hard, they itch like crazy. Rediscovering food was like seeing television for the first time after spending my life listening to the radio.

Sugar was a firework on my tongue. Butter was a sensual, sweating, velvety body, as seductive and undeniable as Elizabeth Taylor. Even the truly indefensible foods—Findus Crispy Pancakes, tinned macaroni & cheese, breakfast pizza—made me feel trashily transgressive, a rebel, a good girl gone bad.

Naturally, I lost my head. I started to gain weight again and struggled to control myself around food. I seemed to have just two settings—nothing or everything all at once! By the time I started university in 2004, I was bigger than I wanted to be.

Looking back, I know that it was my relationship with food that was the issue, not my size. The former hadn't been resolved at all.

I had to build a path to the place where I could feel good about my body, and work out how to nourish it properly. I discovered that it was down to me to choose the right fuel, and remember that a little of what I fancied would always do me good, but a whole packet of Wagon Wheels would make me feel nauseous, edgy, and incapable of having a solid shit for a week. Even now, when I feel a little lost and can't silence the chorus of inner voices shouting, "Are you SURE you want to eat that? Go on, where's the harm in it? But how will you feel afterwards?" I ask myself if I'd give it to my imaginary eight-year-old child. How was it prepared? Does it have any real nutritional value? Is it loaded with enough sugar and caffeine to keep me up for a month? It's not a perfect method, but it generally steers me in the direction of a diverse and nourishing diet.

However, it's very hard to listen to yourself and stay calm when there are so many free-floating thoughts, opinions and conspiracies concerning our bodies and what we feed them.

Every advert and article potentially has polluting properties, wrecking our hard-won equilibrium and forcing us to question everything. I remember one friend despairing when she saw a commercial for cracked-heel cream. "I don't think I'd ever given a second's consideration to my heels," she wailed. "It might have been the one part of my body that I'd never criticized or complained about, mainly because no one had ever asked me to scrutinize it. I don't want sexy heels. I just want my feet to be left in peace! But now I'm paranoid about them, and I don't even know which bit of my body they want me to hate first anymore! Should I keep worrying about my stomach and my arse, or focus on minimizing the inevitable crows' feet before they start? I have a full-time job! The ad people have started to make me feel as though I ought to get up early to worry about things!"

I spend a lot of time feeling this way. I just checked my emails and the most recent thing to hit my inbox was an offer for a discounted "face freezing" course. Often, I'm filled with despair when I see a beautiful body that looks nothing like mine, only to realize that I'm staring at a "before" picture.

There's an increasingly loud group of voices demanding that we fight the power, end the body fascism and refuse to give our money to the marketeers who know that the way to our wallets is through our ploughed, diminished self-esteem.

It's wonderful that people recognize that there's a problem and want to address it, but it can be overwhelming, too. We're told to fight for all womenkind, destroy the system and challenge everything we have been taught for the greater good of all. But, some days we really just want to be able to walk down the street in our favorite clothes, and enjoy the way we look and feel without fearing it's all wrong. We're too fat, unhealthily thin, scruffy, trying too hard, showing too much leg, not celebrating our curves, weirdly pale, overly fake-tanned, boringly dressed, pretentiously eccentric, and letting the feminist side down because we're wearing pink trainers.

Our bodies are battlegrounds, and to be a woman in the twenty-first century is to be constantly stressed and strung out because everyone is constantly trying to lay claim to your territory. At thirteen, listening to all those opinions broke me down and literally diminished me. At thirty-one, I've been able to put myself back together in a mature and orderly fashion—screaming, "Shut up! SHUT UP! No one CARES what you think!" even if I'm just shouting it at a well-meaning stranger on the television, who's telling me about fine lines and wrinkles.

One thrilling, comforting change I have noticed is the way that women are slowly changing their attitude to exercise.

When you grow up feeling fat and desperately self-conscious, trying to exercise in public feels like entering yourself in a freak show and being so confident of your impending, dramatic humiliation that you buy your own giant red rosette. P.E. was to be avoided, as it gave my punchers inspiration and ammunition. Then, when I had an eating disorder and was in a position to articulate the hatred I felt for my own body, sport was the stick I used to beat myself with. I despised exercise, but I despised myself more, so the stationary bike and the leg press were my punishments for being less than perfect. But as I became an adult, I noticed more and more people doing sport for fun! What was behind this mysterious movement? Why were people I knew and liked canceling pub trips to play netball?

I heard rumors that exercise wasn't just an endurance test, a thing you had to put your body through in order to make it slightly more socially acceptable. There were stories of endorphins, and of a sense of growing satisfaction that you experienced as your muscles became stronger. I was convinced that this had to be bullshit—but not so convinced that I didn't want to try it for myself, just to check.

First, I tried Bikram yoga, because I could pretend that I was doing it for entirely spiritual reasons and didn't just want to be a bit thinner. I was amazed that, by day six, my body was capable of moves and poses that I couldn't have drawn on a piece of paper with a biro on day one. Also, I found that extreme dehydration and a carton of coconut water made me crazily high. My heart was flooded with a new-found love for my body, especially my hands. I couldn't stop staring and smiling at them after class. Then I joined a gym and was amazed at how much sweat I was capable of producing. Truly shocked and delighted. My eyelids. The backs of my knees.

Even my heels. How clever my body was! How efficient!

I avoided running, because I was so sure I couldn't do it, and then, one brave day, I tried and learned that I could! My curiosity about my body's capabilities battled my sense of self-consciousness, and won. I don't run because it makes me thinner or hotter. I run because it means that for at least half an hour of the day I'm not worrying about weight loss—I'm busy counting leaf shapes, different shades of green in the trees, and trying to identify bird song. (Running might not change the way you look but it will turn you into a total hippy.)

Exercise is one of the techniques that makes my anxiety disorder much easier to control. When I put pressure on my body, I take it off my brain. My body has never been the problem, but if I've ever blamed it for my own unhappiness, it's because I was looking at it through the wrong lens in my head.

Some people don't want us to feel good about our bodies—it makes us strong when we're more useful to them when we're weak. When women realize they don't need to be sexy, or attractive, or decorative, and can be powerful in other ways, on their own terms, they frighten people and become socially disruptive. So whole organizations and industries have a vested interest in keeping our confidence down and taking our power away. Think of how much you could be achieving if you weren't being drip fed the sort of poisoned thoughts that mean you spend twenty-five minutes staring sadly at salads when you really want a sandwich! Who would lose billions of pounds if you decided that you could be confident and powerful without weight-loss tea and face freezing? But if worrying about your body is a full-time job, fighting the powers that foster the fear means you have to take on a fourteen-hour night shift. After gaining some weight, I wrote a letter to myself about how hard it was to love my body and be kind to it, in order to encourage me to keep trying. Here it is:

Dear Daisy

Shall we talk about your body?

Your body, which used to be thinner. Which you took for granted, because it fitted into cheap, tight dresses. Your body, which took you up and down Brixton Hill, every day, twice a day, never unheralded by catcalls, the stream of men and their, "Oh baby, hey baby, nice tits, nice ass, hey WHERE YOU GOING?"

Your body was a girl's body, made from dancing and late nights and skipped dinners, of hopefulness and sleeplessness and sadness. It took care of itself, or rather, you didn't care that it couldn't. It wasn't for you, and so you didn't mind that you couldn't always afford to feed and nurture it. The admiration of others was nourishment enough. You often went to bed feeling empty. You thought it was heartbreak.

It was probably hunger.

Then your body became plump with love.

Late dinners and later breakfasts, cream in your coffee, champagne in the bath, room-service bacon sandwiches.

Watching your skin, glowing and gold, buttocks round on white sheets, talking and kissing and laughing, the tension in your stomach dissipating.

Love gave you the confidence to grow your career. And your body grew with it. Writing in bed, writing on sofas, writing at the kitchen table, your body still so your brain could pump thoughts furiously, fingers flying.

Now, you have the body you deserve. The body of a woman in love, who is loved, who's managing to make money and maintain a room of her own. A woman who adores buying wickedly extravagant dinners for people she likes, and has the wherewithal for a cab home afterwards. A woman with wide hips and full thighs, who can't pour herself inside the cheap, tight dresses any more.

And even though you have everything to be confident about, everything to play for, this has made you sad. You worry that in spite of everything you have gained, the world liked you more when you took up less space.

It's hard to be honest about how you feel, how you worry sometimes that even though you're bigger, you're disappearing, how dressing up was once a source of joy and it's now a source of panic, how it's hard fully to appreciate why zips get stuck and buttons don't meet in the middle.

And everyone says "love your body", but it's an empty instruction, like 'fly a kite!' It sounds wonderful, but it's hard, and confusing, and you feel guilty because you can't get it right.

You don't have to love your body all the time. But love it in bed, and in the bath. Love it when you're walking fast, and your music is loud, and your boots are clumpy. Love it when you're walking up huge, hidden gym hills, and the sweat burns your eyelids, and you still, somehow, keep going. Love the way your belly shakes when you laugh, and your legs shake when you orgasm, and your shoulders shake when you cry. Keep taking vitamins and washing your face carefully. Dance more, dance harder, and don't stop downing a pint of water after the wine, before you go to sleep.

Feel thankful. Turn your thoughts around. When you catch yourself feeling sad, or scared, or angry, stop and breathe. Think about how badly you'd miss it if you didn't have it. Remember the places it has taken you, the problems it has helped you solve, the delicious meals you have eaten with it, the magical music and exquisite visions it has made you appreciate.

But mostly, don't worry. As long as you can sing and come and giggle and wiggle and weep, you're treating your body exactly as you're supposed to.

Love, Gorgeous you

We forget to think about just how clever our bodies are. Regardless of how much you weigh and the number on the label of your jeans, you own and operate something that can potentially orgasm by itself, make a cup of tea, read a map (or follow the blue dot on a GPS system), dance the Macarena, recite jokes, recall entire episodes of *The Simpsons*, cook a risotto, sing along to the radio, buy insurance, get through airport security, finish *War and Peace*, fart, hiccup, giggle, and burp! We learn, we grow, we remember! We have an up there for thinking, and a down there for dancing. If any part of our bodies works in some helpful, useful way, we're magical miracle robots. Being negative about our bodies puts a strain on all of our parts. It slows us down, forces us to stay in first gear and stops us from flying.

Tilda was diagnosed with severe early onset arthritis four years ago.
She says:

*I have never loved my body or appreciated it more than I do
now. When I think about my early twenties and the way I treated it, I don't know whether to laugh or cry.*

*Obviously, I could have done more exercise, avoided alcohol
and not gone on all those nights out that ended at 5 a.m.—but I
wouldn't have changed a moment. I wish, with all my heart, that
I had loved it better, and treated it, and me, with more kindness.
I did not know what I had, and I spent so much time wishing I
was thinner, doing stupid crash diets, eating crisps, and hating
myself more with every mouthful.*

*I was in a pub recently, and overheard two young women in
the loos. Both were gorgeous, I'd guess they were about twenty-five, and they were complaining about their rolls of flab and
talking about the South Beach diet. Being healthy is obviously
really important, but there's no point making yourself miserable
by spending a fortnight avoiding bread when you could be out
there celebrating the fact that you have two arms, two legs, and
everything works!*

I think my body changed even more in my twenties than it did
when I was in my teens. I still get hair in funny places—I'd like a
shout-out for the mysterious, dark wiry hair that shoots out of my
chin every six to eight weeks. My arse is bigger than it has ever been,
but rounder and higher, too. I have new muscles, and thicker, shinier
hair, because I make enough cash to see a decent stylist instead of trying to do it myself with Sun-In and nail scissors. I know what my body
likes (sex, avocados, solid LOLs) and what it dislikes (comedowns,
hangovers, pointy shoes with high heels that are so painful I have to

do the breathing techniques I helped a friend to learn before she went into labor).

I've spent the last ten years not just trying to love my body—I've been learning to live in it. Our bodies are our homes. We need to feel welcome within them. We don't have to worry about making the beds or doing the dishes as long as we can light some candles, feel comfy on the sofa and choose the pictures we hang on the walls.

DAISY DOES THIS!

➤ I tell myself, "Work with the body you have today!" This is a phrase I hear every time I go to yoga, and it means that our bodies and their capabilities change constantly. If I'm not feeling good about my body, I gently remind myself that I'm not a statue, and being tired, hormonal or run down might be making me feel bad about myself—but I need to love my body hard for twenty-four hours and remember that I'll feel completely different tomorrow.

➤ I ignore clothes sizes. Worrying about being a certain size only makes me miserable, so I remind myself that I can sometimes be three different sizes in the same shop, on the same day. Gorgeousness has no numeric value.

➤ I focus on the good things I do for my body. In the past, I've emotionally beaten myself up for gorging on chips—so I consciously think, "Well done for going on that run!" "Good girl for eating all those vegetables!" It sounds silly, but it makes me smile—and it makes me want to eat more vegetables, which can only be positive.

➤ I like to spend at least five minutes applying my favorite scented body lotion. I focus on how soft my skin feels, how good it smells and how I'm enjoying the sensation of touch.

A Few Words About...

Washing Your Hair

I learned how to wash my hair properly when I was twenty-nine years old.

I wasn't surfing a wave of scurf and grease, or anything—and I definitely wasn't one of those bold, confident people who say, "I heard that your hair washes itself if you leave it for six weeks! So, I thought I'd give it a go!" I rubbed my hair with shampoo and smothered it with conditioner every two days. I spent money I didn't have on it, hoping for a miracle, thinking that the right hairdresser could fix it, and fix me—if my hair was silky and smooth, I could be too—while the brittle, fried knots I was living with represented a personal failing. I dreaded washing my own hair, and worse, drying it, because being on my own with my hair meant being on my own in my head. It was a chore to rush so that I could get on with the business of distracting myself from myself.

Then I met Ian.

He was recommended to me by a glamorous person I didn't know very well, a silky, smooth-seeming person. I believed Ian could fix me, transform me, and help me escape myself, head first. Ian was very expensive, which sat well with my insecure conviction that if I can't afford something, I probably really need it. And Ian was rude about my hair.

"It's in appalling condition," he sniffed, picking up a strand that was attached to a clump that was turning into a dreadlock. "I suppose you shampoo it once and then comb the conditioner through with your fingers."

There was another way?

"Ian, I'm very busy. I have a lot of hair."

Of course, he had time for elaborate, hair-based rituals—he was hanging out with hair all bloody day long. I had a packed schedule! If I spent too long on personal grooming, how would I make time to say yes to everything that everyone else wanted me to do? Or get any self-loathing done?

"I wouldn't treat a hat the way you treat your hair."

I sat and sulked silently for a few minutes. I didn't deserve good hair. I didn't deserve good anything. It was a follicular representation of my earthly value. For a day or so, I'd have a smooth, beautiful blowout and then the facade would crack and I'd be left with a tangled mess. Like my career, my finances, my love life—it might look good for a limited period, and then I'd be left with unmanageable tangles because I didn't deserve any better.

Ian was the first person to tell me the methodology behind good hair. As I sipped champagne (Ian is anti-prosecco) he explained that the chemicals that make shampoo lather are the ones that dry your hair out, the first round of shampooing just loosens the dirt and the second actually gets your hair clean.

He said that unless I combed through the conditioner with a proper device, I might as well sing my hair a lullaby in order to make it soft and manageable. Perhaps because I looked like I was about to cry, Ian softened. "Lots of girls would kill for hair as thick as yours. But no one has good hair unless they put the work in. Take better care of it, and it will take care of you." According to Ian, I could no longer blame my crappy hair, and by extension, my crappy life, on bad luck.

At the time, the idea of taking care of anything was daunting. I was a plant-murdering, dinner-skipping, overdraft- charge-accumulating disaster. But Ian gave me a small project. He believed in me. So, I ended up in TK Maxx buying bargain sulfate-free shampoo. It sparked a tiny revolution that started on my head, but became body wide. Every time I stood in the shower, pouring a second measure of shampoo into my palm, I'd think, "However badly you fucked up today, you are washing your hair like an adult!"

A couple of months later I returned to Ian. He was pleased by my measurable progress. I started to investigate the world of masques, occasionally combing a fistful of goop through my hair before going to the gym. Every deadline I met and vegetable I ate seemed to add a brick to this new path I was building—the road to becoming A Sensible Adult Woman With Nice Hair.

If you've ever had a bath or a cup of tea, you'll understand the humble, healing powers of hot water, and standing under a shower feeling my dirty hair becoming clean seems like nothing less than a rebirth. For too long, washing my hair had reminded me of the Sunday night scent of soap, salvation, and school in the morning. The weekly hair wash was the worst kind of ritual. My little sisters would try to resist it, I'd be begged to set a good example and we'd all leave the tub smelling of Head and Shoulders. It was about doing the bare minimum. Cleanliness had everything to do with decency and nothing to do with personal vanity.

When I was old enough to be responsible for keeping my own hair clean, it was all I could do to endure the chore. Even as an adult I couldn't bring myself to make time for it, or for me.

But when I started washing it under Ian's instructions, I started to feel lots of surprising things—it was OK to be on my own for an hour and in a place where I couldn't instantly reply to messages and emails; it was OK to be naked, and look at my body without shielding my eyes as I got used to the sight of my knees, shins, and nipples; I probably wouldn't leave the shower with shampoo-advert hair, but it was mine and that was enough. It was a basic place to start, but the good feelings trickled down like warm water on my bare back.

If you're feeling low, and want to feel loved, stop what you're doing and wash your hair like this.

You will need:
   A sturdy comb Shampoo Conditioner Hot water
   A soft towel
   An hour, and patience

1. Step under the warm water, and take a little shampoo in the palm of your hand. Use both hands to rub it vigorously into your scalp. Be firm. You're using the heat and strength of your hands to smooth every scary, pointy thought in your head. Rub until your hands ache, and rinse.

2. Do it again. This time, the shampoo should foam only a little. Think about how thorough your work is—you're not just moving the dirt around, you're sending it down the drain. Months, if not years, of lingering bad dates and mean friends and shameful mistakes and other people's cigarettes—all gone now. No more.

3. Squeeze your hair. Divide it into sections, squeeze and squeeze again. Get all the water out. Now take your comb (my preferred brand is a Tangle Teaser) and prepare for battle. This is the hardest bit. You're running up a hill. You're taking on Godzilla. But, if you can do this, and comb out all the knots, you're one step closer to speaking up in a meeting, or telling your bad boyfriend to fuck off, or opening that terrifying envelope on the doormat.

4. This is the fun part! Give your hair a final squeeze, and then take the most delicious smelling conditioner you can afford. Section

by section, comb it through. You're fattening the turkey. The follicles are becoming plump and powerful, sucking up all the moisture and nutrition that you're giving them because you followed the rule.

5. Use your fingers to make sure your hair is coated. Give it a final gentle rub. Rinse out all the conditioner with cool water.

6. Wrap it in a towel, and dry it very gently, if at all. It's clean. It smells good. No matter what comes before or after, at this moment you have the cleanest, softest hair in the universe.

Giving hair-washing instructions might seem more obvious and condescending than launching a food blog with a recipe for beans on toast. What wasn't obvious to me was that the way we choose to take care of ourselves often has a bigger impact than the one you immediately see on the surface. I don't have the grandest, glossiest hair in the world—but I do have a sense that in one tiny area, I'm nourished, healthy, and doing my very best. No one benefits from it but me. We all need to find spaces to be that selfish—because that's when we work out how to be alone with ourselves, and at peace with ourselves.

You could learn to cook a gastronomically ambitious range of dinners for one, or memorize a poem in a barely known ghost language that you recite only when no one is around. Be wildly ambitious in your selfishness! But, it doesn't do you any harm to start with really clean hair.

CHAPTER SEVEN

How To Be Healthy (In Body And Mind)

For the last couple of years, we've been collectively obsessed with health and "wellness". While anything that promotes a better understanding of our bodies, and makes us eat more vegetables, is probably a good thing, I think that we've been confused by a series of conflicting messages, which have led a lot of us to lose our understanding of what will bring us health and happiness, and we've started to believe that we can make everything better by knocking back a shot of pomegranate extract when really we just need to have a nap, make a cup of tea, and call our mums.

It's only recently that I've started to understand my health and take it seriously. At the beginning of my twenties, I didn't understand that "healthy" could be anything but a code for "thin". I thought "bad" foods were the ones you loved but had to feel guilty about, and "good" foods were the ones you hated but would make you skinny (while they left you feeling gnawingly hungry). At twenty, I'd never have chosen a salad simply because I fancied it. I've always suspected that the popularity of supermarket sushi has something to do with the way we look to our food to define us, morally and spiritually. Sandwiches are obviously bad, but after a hard morning in the office avoiding bake sales and other people's holiday chocolates, we can't quite face a bowl full of undressed leaves, but we can have a tiny portion of sticky rice, improbably wrapped around a dollop of tuna mayonnaise!

I also thought that being "healthy" didn't extend further than having some sort of tortured eating regime. I didn't really know about self-care, and how it encompasses everything from bathing recreationally to going to the dentist. This is how bad I was at looking after myself:

I have been seriously short-sighted since I was eight years old. I spent my childhood wearing glasses, each pair less flattering than the one before it. I'd tried contact lenses, and at the time the pronounced curvature of my eyeball meant that the only ones I could wear were the size and texture of plastic bottle tops.

So, when I went away to university, I stopped bothering. No one could make me wear my glasses, or go to the dentist, or visit the health center. After my parents stopped sending me, I didn't see a dentist until I was twenty-nine. (Well, I might have seen one without knowing, at supermarkets and train stations, but that's how old I was when I allowed one to look at my teeth.)

I spent three years squinting at people and pushing my face close to the thing I needed to see in the mistaken belief that this was a good look—and better than admitting I desperately needed visual aids. A friend told me that he'd seen me squinting around the campus and had privately nicknamed me "hunchback girl" because I looked like an evil fairytale crone beckoning innocent woodland creatures to come closer.

Essentially, I was in the throes of an unbecoming adolescent rebellion, but I wasn't prepared to break the rules that had been set for me until there was no chance that I could be told off. The trouble with self-care is that it feels a bit parental, at first. Most of it is about remembering to do things that are tedious, or time consuming, or make you look like a bit of an idiot. If we're really lucky, we grew up with a parent or guardian who wanted us to finish our dinners and wear clean clothes, and at some point (for me, it was around the time I turned twenty-five) the penny drops—they weren't doing it to be total fun sponges who wanted us to live joyless lives that centered around the picking up of wet towels. Teaching self-care is an act of love, and most of us squander that love, testing our boundaries, making bad choices and refusing to fix our fillings until we have to phone home and say, "Mum? I might have scurvy."

In a way, I think this is as it should be. Most of us learn that we have a duty of care to ourselves only if we try things the teenage way and slowly realize that we miss vegetables and vitamins. Only by neglecting myself did I discover how complicated health is and that it's not about sometimes selecting a salad that leaves you feeling hungry and grumpy. It's the most boring, prosaic stuff in the world—clean underwear, clean teeth, and a regular bedtime. It means making choices that nourish us, and a Big Mac is sometimes much more nourishing than a three-day juice fast.

After making some seriously unhealthy choices, I learned that it's impossible to feel well unless you've worked to lay down the foundations for some proper wellness. If you're tired, stressed and anxious, you're going to make some weird decisions, like spending a month's wages on filling the fridge full of bee pollen, or thinking you can fix yourself by eating nothing but fruit. You're much more likely to act in your own best interests on a full stomach and a solid eight hours' sleep.

I finally bought some proper glasses before I graduated, when my mum gently pointed out that if I were to get a job, there was a good chance that my ability to do that job would be enhanced if I could see at a greater range than "six inches from my face". I refused to wear the glasses on nights out, and I think that decision played a bigger part than alcohol in most of my bad romantic choices. (It sounds very shallow, but I'd never have pursued that Nazi goth metal fan if I could have read the band name written on his T-shirt.) I finally had another go with contact lenses when my good friend and deskmate Zoe exploded with friendly rage when, one fine payday, I was thinking about spending some hard-earned cash on an expensive meal replacement service, which promised to make my skin glow. (It was guaranteed to work, because your face would go pink with terror every time you remembered that you spent £200 on it.)

"Daisy. Honey. Please take whatever money you intend to spend on these tiny grey bottles of nonsense and go to the sodding optician, please. You need contact lenses, or glasses that you can wear in clubs, because I can't take another night of watching you trying to read large print cocktail lists and peering at every blond man you see in a VIP section and asking me if it's one of the Hemsworth brothers."

Slowly, I started to realize that perhaps I'd been confusing health with vanity. I had been making my life so much harder for myself than it needed to be. To use the cheesiest and clunkiest of metaphors, when I got contact lenses, I started to see clearly where I had been going wrong. For a long time, I'd thought that I couldn't afford the extra £20 a month, but I wasn't nearly so circumspect about my finances when buying bottles of bad wine.

My friend Marla explains how her own relationship with "wellness" has evolved over time:

For a while, I thought that I was "balanced" because I was sober in the week, but really went for it at the weekends. I know that to some extent, that feels quite natural. You want to feel healthy when you have to be at work, but then relax in your own time. But I didn't do it in a healthy way. I'd instigated a "no alcohol, no carbs" weekday rule, but existing on protein and leaves meant I was exhausted, and furious with everyone, come 4 p.m. If someone in the office had a birthday, I'd be an-gry with myself if I accidentally ate any cake. Then, as soon as Friday rolled around I'd be texting my dealer while I worked my way through a bottle of prosecco at my desk. I said yes to every single invite because, hello, it's the weekend!

But living that lifestyle took its toll. Pretty much every Sun-day night, I'd be sobbing into a takeaway because I'd put my body through so much and I felt awful. I thought I could "cure" it with my weekday regime, but I was just placing extra stress on every single part of me. When I was twenty-eight, I was off work for three months with anxiety and depression, and started seeing a counsellor, who got me to talk about my issues around food, "wellness" and control. She helped me to reframe totally how I saw health, and to understand that I might be calmer and happier if I had a Mars Bar on a Wednesday if I fancied it, or stayed in on Friday night and had a bath if I was worn out from the week. It sounds so obvious now! But everyone around me at work had a vaguely similar regime. I genuinely thought I was one of the healthiest people I knew because I drank so many cold-pressed juices, but I wasn't nourishing myself at all.

I was in my mid-twenties when I truly realized that health comes from the inside out, and that it's impossible to nourish your body unless you're nourishing your mind first.

It was the winter before my twenty-sixth birthday, and I felt sick. I experienced a sharp pain in my left shoulder blade every time I leaned forward to pick up my office phone. I felt badly nauseous for the first hour of every morning of every day, and I'd peed on enough sticks to know that the answer

wasn't the obvious one. The worst feeling of all was indefinable, a sensation that seemed to feature in every serious French novel, only for the specific word to get lost in translation. I was filled with a constant sense of panic and despair that was growing and physical, as if someone had implanted my body with a balloon, and was inflating it with more dread every day.

Nothing was obviously wrong, yet I felt as though I was always on the brink of bursting into tears. I'd made an appointment to see my physician, ostensibly about the back pain, but really hoping for a magic cure for my impossible panic. I'd seen him before, a nervous middle-aged man who seemed slightly scared of his own stethoscope. How could he help? I didn't want to go. I wanted to lie at the side of the road and sob.

"All you have to do," I told myself sternly, "is to keep putting one foot in front of the other." Somehow, I kept walking.

When I was little, I loved the story of Chicken Licken.

Chicken Licken is a chicken, obviously, and she has a coterie of avian pals with similarly descriptive, rhyming names. (This caused consternation when one of my sisters made an incorrect yet logical guess about what the duck might be called.) An acorn hits Chicken Licken on the head, and she thinks this means that the sky is falling down, and so goes to alert the relevant authorities, telling her friends along the way. They meet a fox who, in the version I was told, suggests that everyone takes shelter in his lair. They go, despite the fact that nothing good ever happens in a lair, and the fox kills them and eats them. Of course the fox eats them.

So, when I went to the doctor because I felt trapped inside the hell of my own mind and didn't trust myself to boil a kettle without filling in a mental risk assessment form, the words of Chicken Licken bounced around my brain like a particularly irritating advert. "The sky is falling down, and I'm on my way to tell the king!" The anxiety was making me so illogical that I believed there was a chance I might get eaten by a fox along the way.

When my anxiety disorder is very bad, I feel like I've been drinking cheap instant coffee cut with cheaper speed. My synapses snap, and the regular chemical signals that course through them are replaced by popping candy. Anxiety is the "what if " disease—I'm acutely aware of every single potentially disastrous variable and trying to prevent them all as ineptly as King Canute holding back the tides with a flannel.

It's really hard. But our bodies and minds don't always work as well as we want them to, and while it's good to learn how we can look after ourselves, we can't always heal ourselves. Finding the strength to speak to a doctor about my feelings of depression and anxiety didn't stop my sadness, but it lessened as I learned to take my mental health as seriously as my physical health.

I was on the brink of a breakthrough with my anxiety disorder, as I started to realize it was something that I'd never be cured of—I had to live with it. In the last few years it had flared up, got better, buzzed in the background and then reached a roaring crescendo once more. In time, I'd learn from this and make all sorts of wise observations about prioritizing and maintaining my mental health. But, at that moment, my world was ending, the crops were failing and everyone I loved might die imminently, unless they'd swerved a brush with mortality by deciding that they secretly hated me.

When I was 100 meters from the surgery, I thought about how I shouldn't have left my apartment, because something bad would inevitably happen during the half hour that I was away from it. When I was 50 meters from the surgery, I thought about all the people waiting with broken bones, infections and issues that gave their health concerns legitimacy—and how I was taking up valuable time and resources just by ringing up and bothering the receptionist. When I wasn't thinking obsessively about the falling sky, my train of thought was dominated by a percussive "I can't, I can't, I can't". Not crying for long enough to give my name at the desk was too hard. Explaining that I was constantly deafened by the noise of shrill, high-pitched panic battling with the heavy bass note of doom was too hard. Being alive was too hard.

Yet some tiny seed of hope stopped me from going home, or just curling into a ball at the side of the street (which would have been my first preference). Just as I thought that everything was in a state of bottomless free fall, part of me knew I had to carry on surviving for five seconds at a time and keep walking forward.

Twenty minutes later, when I left the surgery with a new prescription and the recommendation that I find a therapist, I started to feel a little bit lighter—not because the doctor had proved to me that I had absolutely nothing to worry about, or I thought that the new batch of anti-depressants would make me skip, sing and feel the urge to get LOVING LYFE!!! tattooed on my inner thigh, but because after spending weeks wading through a thick fog of impending doom, a tiny shot of optimism had cut through my clouds. To use the most middle- class analogy in the world, it was like watching a splash of balsamic vinegar breaking up a puddle of olive oil. I felt good because I had done something for myself. I'd been scared, I'd felt strange, but I'd eventually been able to look up and ask for help. As I found the strength to start spending more time on taking care of myself, it suddenly hit me that this was what being healthy was all about. I was discovering that being truly healthy requires a lot of time, compassion and self-love, and juice cleanses and chia seeds are optional.

Now I see my therapist once every couple of weeks. She's my third. There was the lovely National Health Service one who gave me six, helpful, free sessions when I was first diagnosed. There was the one who ran the group therapy sessions I was referred to a few years later, when the anxiety flared up again. She reminded me so much of the school dinner ladies who were forced to spend a solid lunch hour yelling at the naughty boys for throwing their peas. And there is Katherine, who lets me cry, laugh, swear and criticize people as much as I need to, and her only instruction is usually that I stop second guessing myself and don't caveat my thoughts with, "I *know* I shouldn't think this". Presumably, Katherine would be a bit more forceful if my thoughts were more destructive or genuinely murderous, but knowing that, every two weeks, I can go to her office and let rip is a luxury. She's like an ambitious detective from a kids' cartoon. "No problem too big, no problem too small, just tell her and she'll solve it all!"

A part of me is whispering, "Shhh, dude! Pipe down! Why are you telling everyone that you have mental problems?" But a larger, louder part is yelling, "WOOOOOH, THERAPY! SPREAD THE WORD!" Of all the things I have done for my health, therapy is definitely the best.

If I had an unlimited budget, once I'd bought myself a Hermès Constance handbag and hosted a huge puppy party with an open bar, I'd like to treat the world to a few sessions on the couch. I don't believe that there's anyone who wouldn't feel stronger and more positive about life with the help of a good therapist.

Therapy is a difficult area because it's underfunded, stigmatized, and not always well-regulated. Asking for help is hard, and even if you're brave enough to request it, you might find yourself on a waiting list for a while, although it's possible to shop around if you go private, and rates vary. There are different kinds of therapy, too. CBT (cognitive behavioral therapy) is one of the most popular for treating anxiety and depression. It doesn't necessarily address your issues at their root, but it does look at how you respond to them, and aims to help you discover better coping methods. You might not know what's going to work for you straight away, of course. Almost everyone sees more than one therapist before they find someone they're comfortable with—just go with your gut and remember that it's not like going to an exercise class. If it doesn't feel good, you're allowed to stop immediately.

When we become adults, at least in the technical sense, it can be a real shock to discover that we're responsible for our own health and wellbeing, but it can be the beginning of a really positive relationship, too. It's our responsibility to start working out what's best for us, which might be completely different from the things we were brought up with.

Self-care has been badly branded, and sometimes we call it "pampering". If ever I'm struggling with an upset stomach and I feel the need to trigger some projectile vomiting, I like to mutter the phrase "pampering session" over and over until I'm so nauseated that I start retching involuntarily. Pampering is simultaneously sexless and creepy. It invokes doing complicated things with oils, massages administered by terrifying professionals with tight ponytails, cheap chocolate and sweet prosecco, and sickly pink birthday cards urging "Why not get together with the girls?" It doesn't reflect the need to nurture your human spirit, nor our need for rest, calm and pleasure. If your best method of self-care involves cupcakes and cava, you do you—but to me the worst part of "pampering" is that it sounds like something selfish and unnecessary, when proper self-care is as important as eating and sleeping.

It can be going to the gym with a hair masque on, and powering way up the treadmill with a head that smells of soap and sweat. It can be going to bed with a bag of chips. At its core, it's about identifying what's in the Venn diagram overlap between what you want and what you need, and making sure that you're doing something from that part of the circle at least weekly—ideally every day.

Over the last few years, I've experimented with a few different forms of self-care (kale smoothies, internet shopping, meditation, and Netflix binging) and my current favorite is getting my nails done. Manicures are expensive and last for just a couple of weeks, but I like making it a priority and managing my budget in order to make sure that I can spend money on a tiny thing that brings me pleasure. I like choosing unconventional colors, fluorescent pinks and pastel blues and metallic violet with the depth and sheen of the foil you find on a chocolate bar wrapper. I like that being in the salon forces me to stop looking at my phone for an hour, because I can't use my hands.

My friend Ali tells me that painting her own nails is a crucial part of her own self-care. "It's a ritual, and I love being at home with a bowl of water, the towels out and the TV on. Doing it myself makes me feel like I'm looking after myself," she explains. Successful self-care isn't about ticking boxes, or doing anything that comes with a "should" attached. You just have to keep trying until you find the thing that feels good.

We're so used to hearing the message that self-control is everything, and we learn to believe that we can't trust our own bodies to tell us what we need, when they're the only voice that we should be listening to. In terms of managing my own health, one of my biggest breakthroughs has been the realization that I need sleep. If I feel as though the world is ending, there's a good chance that everything will look a little less bleak after I've had a nap.

I dream of sleep. To sleep regularly and sufficiently makes you calm, brings you joy, and enables you to scale the very heights of your own potential, to become a source of beauty, happiness and positive power. Sleep is simply amazing. If someone told me that I could sacrifice a family member in order to guarantee myself sufficient, uninterrupted nightly sleep for the rest of my life, I'd think about it. I'd never drink wine again. I'd give up the internet forever.

Admittedly, if I'm serious, I probably ought to give up booze and smartphones. Alcohol has a bad effect on the quality of our sleep, and although it can make us drowsy, when it wears off, a few hours after we've been to bed, the withdrawal takes us from a state of deep sleep and back to REM (rapid eye movement) sleep—the first stage, which is much easier to wake from. This is why I struggle to sleep through the night if I've had more than two drinks. We all know that knocking back three Jägerbombs in a row isn't going to do much to promote feelings of Zen-like calm the next morning, but even too much wine with dinner can wake me up at 4.30 a.m. with a vague, sweaty sense of impending doom.

Similarly, our smartphones emit blue light—this isn't a lead-in for a conspiracy theory, I promise—which has a short wavelength that suppresses melatonin, a hormone that promotes sleepiness. Blue light sends a message to our brain that is interpreted as, "Oi! Morning! Get the coffee on!" Many of us are drinking less, for the sake of our health—but if you're tucked up in bed looking at an Instagram feed full of wellness celebrities, in search of inspiration for tomorrow's breakfast, you might not be setting yourself up for the healthy start you're hoping for.

I've struggled to stay off social media before I go to sleep, especially because of my fascination with sleep tech. There are apps to send you to sleep, apps to measure the quantity and quality of your sleep, apps for power naps, and something called "Yoga for Insomnia". My relationship between my phone and my sleeping habits has become symbiotic. At times I haven't slept because I was obsessively following a Twitter war between two obscure US reality stars, or I was being trolled by someone who thinks I'm fat, or I hadn't turned off my WhatsApp notifications. I'd find myself awake hours after going to bed, feeling panicky and irritated. I'd search for an app to soothe me and send me to sleep, when I really needed to turn my phone off and put at least two doorways between it and me. A damaging addiction is one where you can't stop using something even though it's harming your life. I wouldn't make myself a nightcap from Red Bull and ground-up Pro Plus, or try to feel calm and ready for rest with a noisy game of *Fortnite* immediately before bed, so why did I keep doing this to myself? After all, I knew the benefits of waking up rested.

We give our phones so much power because they have such a big presence in our lives. We can sleep better if we take small steps to diminish that presence and stop relying on apps. About a year ago I was arguing with a friend, who claimed that her sleeping patterns were better than they'd been for years since she started leaving her phone in a different room while she slept. I argued that I couldn't possibly do that, because how would I wake up in the morning without an alarm? She looked horrified for a second, then reminded me about old-fashioned alarm clocks, which would get me out of bed without rousing me at 4 a.m. to tell me that Justin Bieber had bought another monkey. Another secret weapon in the battle of Daisy versus sleep has been the bedroom TV. I love to read in bed, but if the book gets too exciting my brain gets overstimulated. However, gloriously boring TV acts like a sleeping pill, without any of the side effects. (Sleep medication gives me a hangover and makes me incredibly clumsy the day afterwards). Television screens also emit blue light, and most sleep experts would advise that you watch bedtime TV in moderation for that reason. I think it helps me wind down because it doesn't have the interactive element of social-media use.

No shortcuts help us to stay mentally and physically healthy. Growing up means realizing that it's up to us to look after ourselves, and sometimes that feels like a full-time job. However, it's also an act of love, and every time you listen to your body and mind, and give them what they need, you're acknowledging that you exist and you matter. Everything you do to take good care of yourself is an investment that will give you the best shot at feeling strong, nurtured and happy in years to come.

DAISY DOES THIS!

➤ The first thing is to remember that health begins and ends with mental health. The way I treat my body has a big impact on my mind, and I can only get it right if I start by focusing on my mind, and the way I want to feel.

➤ To me, it's important to do something positive for my mental health every day—and sometimes doing nothing is just as important. Eating broccoli, reading a gripping book, dancing to the radio or having a bath—it's all good as long as it makes you happy for at least five minutes.

➤ Spending money "selfishly" is really important, and I budget for self-care. For me, it's a form of mental-health insurance that keeps me on an even keel.

➤ My phone goes on Airplane mode and lives outside the bedroom between 10 p.m. and 7 a.m., so that it doesn't distract me from getting a good night's rest. Twitter might be the social network that never sleeps, but I need to.

A Few Words About...

Panic Attacks

Panic attacks are terrifying, debilitating, unmanageable, sweaty freak-outs. They are also a writer's dream. The poetic potential of a panic attack is infinite. Even if you're really stuck, there's a strict metaphorical form you can adopt that conveys some impression of the physical sensation of the world ending. Legs are described as being like a very light, insubstantial material (jelly, cotton wool) or something very hard and immovable (lead, granite, porridge cooling on the side of a cereal bowl). The head is full of a flickering, hard-to-stop substance (popping candy, silverfish, static on an old-fashioned television before everything went digital). You sweat rivers, or buckets, or as though you're in a sauna in Southern Europe and you've just started to realize that it's much, much hotter than the one at your local gym. Imagine those stock sexy images of flowers blooming, trains going into tunnels, fountains spurting into life. Then picture every single one of those images exploding into a terrifying death fire that leaves everything charred and sad, like inedible burnt toast. There's your panic attack!

But that isn't right either. It's different for every single person, often every single time. If you struggle with depression or an anxiety disorder, you might experience panic attacks frequently enough to learn to recognize them, but we're all at risk. I don't say that to frighten, but to reassure—in our twenties, when we're getting our first helpings at life's endless stress buffet, we're most likely to experience a series of shocking, surprising symptoms that leave us reeling and wondering, "What was that?"

I'd had a few before I understood what was going on. The first one that I remember happened in my third year of university. I had just got together with my second proper boyfriend, and I really, really liked him, but that made me feel powerless. He was sweet. He was kind. He was straightforward. And I wondered what he was hiding. I'd decided that I needed to play a few games in order to hold his attention, and make him believe I was worthy of him. At the time, deep down, I just couldn't believe that anyone in the world would possibly want me as I was—unless they were a sad, desperate loser, too.

So, I decided to "act casual". Sometimes I pretended that I didn't want to see him. If I bumped into him on a night out, I'd smile and nod, instead of rushing over to make out with him. I should mention that this man was, and is, one of the top three greatest kissers that I've ever had the good fortune to meet. Also, I was so nervous about maintaining my cool, casual persona around him that I would get hammered if I thought I was going to see him. My sophisticated act was unconvincing on a good day, and a lost cause when I was knocking over drinks and falling into tables.

The relationship was hugely, horribly stressful, because I made it so. Also, at the time, I was struggling with my degree, and too frightened even to address how worried I was, let alone confront my fears head on. My grades were low and I felt as though I'd lost my aptitude for study completely. As much as anything, it was a blow to my ego, just like when I started secondary school and felt that being around smart people made me stupid. By the time I'd left school, I'd reclaimed my "clever" crown, but that was all I had. I didn't feel pretty, or cool, or interesting in any other way. I'd gone off to university and had my "clever" removed, and I was on the brink of graduating with several thousand pounds of debt, and a degree that would probably prevent me from getting a decent job. If university made me less of a person, what would the real adult world do to me? Remove my spleen? Prevent me from being able to use my opposable thumbs?

I think that I was pretending that the relationship was the biggest source of stress in my life because my genuine source of stress—a free-floating, nameless terror of a seemingly impossible, unknown, debt- and failure-filled future—was too huge to address, and so I preferred to ignore it when I could (any time that wasn't between 3 a.m. and 5 a.m., when I was usually woken by the dread).

My life was defined by two sets of anxieties, and so one November night, I was alone in my room, reading, when I suddenly felt intensely hot and weepy. Breathing and crying at the same time is always a bit of a struggle, but it became impossible, as if my nose and lungs were filled with lemon seeds. I thought I was going to be sick. I tried to stand up so I could go to the bathroom, but my legs wouldn't hold me up. I collapsed straight back onto the bed. The sweating and nausea made me think that I must have some sort of bug. I felt weak and shaky for about an hour afterwards, but I went to sleep and felt fine the next morning.

I described the events to a friend, who was the first person to use the phrase "panic attack" in relation to what I'd experienced. I felt bewildered, and frightened. Now, there's much more discussion about mental health and anxiety, how to recognize when there's a problem and how symptoms manifest themselves. At the time, I'd got it into my head that a panic attack was something to do with having asthma. "But I have nothing to worry about!" I protested, because as far as I was concerned, this was normal. Endless, worry-based uncertainty was normal. Feeling permanently tense, twitchy and ready for a telling-off was normal. This is why alcohol was invented—drinking was what allowed me to live in the moment and temporarily stop obsessing about my doomed future. Until I felt sick, or passed out, or found myself in a dangerous situation. Now I know that drinking to forget is like trying to slay the Hydra of Lerna. In the morning, there are twice as many heads as before, and they're all ten times as malevolent.

Over the years, I experienced a variety of panic attacks, with a list of symptoms and sensations longer than the list of women who have been bridesmaids for Henry VIII. One was so extreme that I passed out just after my tube train arrived at Golders Green station—I managed to hurl myself through the door and roll onto the concourse before losing consciousness and control of my bowels. Once, I started weeping and hyperventilating in bed, on a Saturday morning, just after I'd instigated some erotic intimacy with my husband. Life with panic attacks can be hard and horrible, but I appreciate that it's also tough to be on the receiving end when the person you're kissing suddenly deposits snot all over your chin. Here are some of the weirdest places that it's happened to me. There is an unexpected boat theme.

The doctor's waiting room, Leeds, 2004. This was shortly before it turned out that I didn't have cervical cancer. What I had was a cervix.

Mannequins Dance Palace, Disney World, Florida, 2006. I became breathless with panic after I thought that my friend's drink might be spiked. It turned out to be a complimentary light-up ice cube. Mannequins was shut down in 2009. I have a bad feeling that these two events are related.

Sainsbury's, Fulford Road, 2007. This happened when I was on the way to a friend's house to check my degree results, after the internet at home had broken. I popped in for a calming bottle of water. The manager found me crying, "I can't deal," with my head in the freezer cabinet. I passed with merit, and got a bad cold.

A London Duck tour bus, in the actual Thames, 2007. I was at the work Christmas day out for my nightmare PR job, and it occurred to me that if anything went wrong, I'd be drowning at the bottom of the river with some of my deadliest enemies. I hyperventilated into my coat sleeve and pretended that I had a mild fear of fish.

My boyfriend's best friend's boat, somewhere in Southampton, 2009. It was a night like a hundred others. We'd been having a lovely time and then suddenly we weren't.

We'd had too much to drink, then my Terrible Boyfriend—the old friend who became my deadly enemy—started screaming and stormed out into the night, leaving me in the berth we were supposed to share. Something snapped. It was just another row – but there were so many rows, and I never knew what they were about, and I felt trapped and alone at the same time. This panic attack was interrupted by the best friend, who had brought a girl back to the boat and wanted me to get out of the berth so that he could have sex in it. I did not move.

Anxiety – it's nature's cock blocker.

HSBC, Edgware Road, London, 2013. For years, I'd been dealing with my anxieties around financial matters by simply not checking my bank statements and bills. I had to transfer some money that had been sent to me by accident, and I couldn't avoid the situation any longer. It took me two attempts to get through the door (I had been sick in a bush *en route*). My account was in credit! This gave me a second panic attack, a bit like an aftershock—but at least I was smiling throughout.

Oscar night, Honolulu, Hawaii, 2016. I woke up at 4 a.m. weeping, with heart palpitations. I still have no idea why. I was on honeymoon! Leo had won! My theory was that the Academy Award celebrants were enjoying such a high volume of high-grade narcotics that I could feel the side effects from thousands of miles away. Who knew it was possible to feel so unrelaxed when you spend a whole day wearing a lei!?!

It has taken me a long time to accept that my body is my friend and isn't out to betray me. It has evolved to send me signals when I need to worry, and sometimes it sends me the wrong ones—"Your card has been declined" is never a sentence you want to hear, but it doesn't require the same physical response as "You are now being chased by a bear". A panic attack is the culmination of too many bad, confusing signals, but it's the most helpful prompt of all. It's my body's way of saying, "I'm sorry, I might have given you some incorrect information. But you must listen to this. Stop, slow down, be kind to yourself. Take some time out. Have a bath. Nothing is as bad as it seems in your imagination. I am slamming the brakes on now, because you need to put yourself first until you're not haunted by the sense that an invisible ninja is following you around with a machine gun."

A panic attack has no respect for time or location. Your body doesn't care if you're at your grandmother's funeral, or if you've just been pulled on stage by Lady Gaga, or if you're about to be proposed to. If it senses that you are truly overwhelmed, it will pump pure adrenaline through your veins, glands and stomach. It helps me to think of them like bad dates. Hell at the time, but the anecdotes are priceless. On the days when you're feeling calm and happy enough to leave your house, your panic-attack chat will make you a big hit at dinner parties.

CHAPTER EIGHT

How To Get Dressed

As a fat, unstylish child, I spent a lot of time dreaming about being a slim and fashionable adult.

When I left home and was allowed to pick my own outfits, I was going to town! There would be opera capes, sequins, shirts with clever slogans, perhaps an Elizabethan ruff (just because!), short dresses, tight dresses, dresses with magical panels that lit up to turn my whole body into a constellation, because when I was a grown-up, we would surely have the technology! I fantasized about a career as a fashion designer, drawing curiously triangular ladies in a lined notebook, with a leaky blue pen. I knew exactly what I'd say in interviews when I was asked about my influences. "My mother was very strict about my clothes, and did her very best to limit my vivid imagination and nascent creativity! But look at me now, Mum! LOOK AT ME NOW!"

Looking back, if I were the parent of a ten year old, I too would be discouraging her from wearing a homemade bin-liner skirt with a tin-foil train on school non-uniform day. I failed to appreciate that my mum wasn't a boring fashion dinosaur who was living to ruin my fun. At the time, she was a woman in her late thirties with six demanding children, and she'd learned how to dress in a way that suited her life and her body. Right now, I'm wearing a version of the uniform that Mum wore around the house—a cream silk shirt tucked into M&S jeans, and sneakers. Admittedly, the sneakers are silver and glittery, and I'm wearing a necklace decorated with a tiny carnival horse.

Between then and now, I've learned that wearing clothes that work with your life isn't selling out—it's sensible. Also, dressing yourself is hard, and it's easy to get lost between your head and your own wardrobe, even if the latter doesn't house a snowy universe full of friendly fauns.

The trouble is that, now more than ever, clothes don't exist just to keep you warm and stop you getting arrested. They're a way of "signaling to your style tribe"! They're supposed to help you create an Instagrammable image. They send a message about your dreams, aspirations, values and politics. They get you hired and, sometimes, fired. It feels like there are more options than ever, and in 2016 it's much easier to dress a range of body shapes on a range of budgets than it was when I was raiding the cupboard under the kitchen sink for fashion supplies. Does this make life easier or harder? Why do I still want to look like Meg Ryan in *When Harry Met Sally* but also Liza Minnelli in *Cabaret* when the received wisdom is that I should have a signature style, and choose between them? Where is the perfect white shirt? How old is too old for jorts? Has anyone else ever scarred themselves wearing a heavily embellished item? Will I ever accept that if I see the words 'layered kimono' I should ignore them and run far away?

It makes sense that dressing in your twenties is difficult, because you're in the throes of a decade-long identity crisis. My clothes and me had a Burton–Taylor style relationship for ages, and it's only relatively recently that we've worked it out and fallen in love all over again. It's hard to work out what to wear when you don't know who you are, and you keep finding yourself in strange situations that feel like badly scripted plays.

When I've been at my most unhappy, I've tried to dress myself in clothes that conceal my personality and feelings, and wondered why peplums and pinstripes didn't make me feel professional and pulled together. For my first job, when I thought it was vital to do an impression of the adult I so clearly wasn't, I bought a long, severe, plain black shift —and was ashamed when I split the seams, my butt exploding out of it like a sausage escaping its casing. My body was so bewildered and angry with me that it was Hulk Smashing my badly chosen clothes. It should have been a massive clue. I was straining to constrain myself, and mentally beating myself into submission in order to try to become the adult I thought I ought to be. I always got it wrong. When I got to *Bliss*, I found myself working in a space where my personality was an asset, not a liability, and over time, I stopped being scared of my own clothes. I could breathe out.

A couple of weird things happened when I worked there. The first was reassuring. While we were committed to being honest with our readers, and didn't airbrush or digitally alter any of our images, I discovered that all sorts of legitimate tricks could be used to make someone look good in a picture.

Standing almost anyone under a professional lighting rig will make them appear lovely and luminous. Clothes are always pinned into place so that stars look amazing from the front, and like a pin cushion from the back. Really talented make-up artists don't just hide your spots and apply non-wobbly eyeliner—they can change a person's bone structure with a bit of powder and a brush. Almost every celebrity I have ever met is half my height and a quarter of my width, and they'd turn up to shoots in cozy jogging bottoms and a hoodie. Sometimes during a shoot, assistants would rush in with a fresh consignment of designer T-shirts, or £3,000 watches. Even during an interview, big celebrities would have, as well as a PR person, assistant and manager, a make-up artist on hand, who would dust their nose between questions, just in case I was thinking about starting my piece with the words "I'm in a hotel suite with *Hollyoaks'* hottest new star, and blimey, her pores are enormous!"

I like to remember all of these things when I'm thinking about a picture of Jennifer Lopez and wondering why there's nothing in my wardrobe that will make me seem as though I'm made of satin and spun platinum. Not even JLo looks like JLo. Unless I'm prepared to find someone who will follow me around with a massive lighting rig, I have to dress for myself and believe I look good for a normal human being—and remember that I'm not expected to appear like a cartoon of a cool, sexy lady because I'm not required to sell any records, shampoo or yoghurt.

The other thing that happened was the social-media explosion.

I started at *Bliss* less than a year after the first iPhone was launched in the UK. I was on Facebook, which, at the time, was used by students and graduates posting blurry, low-resolution pictures of friends drinking dodgy multicolored things through very long straws, or just squinting confusedly at a camera flash. By the time Instagram launched a couple of years later, we were striving to look sexy, not silly, in our own photos. And fashion blogging was invented. "They're just normal people in totally cool clothes!" screamed the press, and I was puzzled.

The bloggers looked like celebrities. They were slim, pretty and perfectly lit, with a seemingly unlimited supply of beautiful new outfits. Some were smart and inspiring, and had a really fascinating perspective on the theory of fashion. I started to feel like I'd missed a memo. What kind of idiot would waste her time accepting that she was never going to look like a model, when everyone else had been out learning to look like models? How could I have ever imagined that buying a pretty dress from Topshop on payday was enough? Suddenly, everyone was expected to be a model and stylist, simultaneously, and I felt completely inadequate. In magazines, fashion is a fantasy and it's easy to accept beauty as a lovely lie. When you're posting pictures to digital platforms alongside stylish "normals", you feel the social media side eye framing your photos like an old-fashioned Polaroid border. I started to feel it was pointless to try to participate in fashion and style—it would be like turning up at the Academy of Fine Arts with a multipack of Crayola crayons.

My fashion freak-out came to a head when I went freelance. For a long time I'd been commuting to the depths of Kent, a place that feels as though it's always winter and never Christmas when you're on a train to it at 7 a.m. Every day I had to put on clothes that felt reasonably stylish and suitable for post-work events but did not prevent me from walking up the series of vertical hills between the station and the office. I could not spend too much time looking at my wardrobe and feeling consumed by style self-loathing, however, since I was barely conscious when my alarm went off.

When I started working from home, in my pajamas, the crisis that had been brewing came to a head. It didn't help that I'd gained weight, my uphill walks having been replaced by waddles to the fridge in the kitchen. I'd been so excited about having the time and space to experiment, work on my style and discover a look that was my own, rather than the version of me that might end the day covered in llama sick after an ill-advised photo shoot with a boy band at a city farm. "I just don't know who I am any more!" I sobbed one day, shaking my fist at a bright pink prom dress as though I'd just found out that it had slept with my boyfriend and my dad. As well as being too big for my clothes for biscuit-related reasons, I felt too old. In my early twenties, it seemed fine to wear cheap shoes and cheaper dresses that showed your knickers if you sneezed. As thirty loomed, my old clothes didn't feel right – but I wasn't ready to return to pinstriped punishment and the black shifts of doom. I wanted "forever pieces"—clothes that felt fancy, luxurious things I could invest in and love forever—but I was terrified of making an expensive mistake, and convinced my taste wasn't good enough to stop me from making a fool of myself.

Eliza, a stylist, says:

Buying fewer things and spending more money on them is actually safer, because it's much easier to resell a high-value item if you decide that it's not for you. On that note, there are so many auction sites, designer consignment shops and places with last-season designer items that it's very easy to track down 'investment pieces' that are a bit more affordable. I have to dress people for work and so I've learned to use social media as a tool for inspiration, not a source of envy. I really analyse the pictures that catch my eye. Is it the colour I love, or the cut? How are people moving or standing in shot? If someone's leaning dramatically to the left, I'll bet you any money that her dress looks strange when she's standing up straight. You don't have to copy anyone's look. Do what you can to break it down, and separate the elements that appeal to you.

Sometimes I'm jealous of someone's outfit, but she's holding a Starbucks cup and standing on Mulberry Street and I realise that what I really want is a coffee and a trip to New York.

As a die-hard *Mad Men* fan, I should know how advertising works. In the western world, our eyes and brains have been trained to respond to any signal of desirability. We see a pretty picture and think "I want!", although as Eliza explains, we can't always work out exactly what it is we want. The fact that our cravings are constantly stimulated means that most of us end up with far too much stuff. My friend Rachel became so overwhelmed by it that she undertook a decluttering mission. It hasn't turned her into a more cautious shopper, though. In fact, the reverse has happened:

I was always freaking out about what to wear, because I could never bloody find anything. Occasionally, I'd haul things out of my wardrobe, throw them on the bed, feel consumed with guilt about my western ways and my collection of cheap clothes I hated and couldn't really afford, and then bundle everything back in again. I'd fantasize about house fires, and being forced to start all over again with five perfectly chosen items. Eventually, someone gave me a book about decluttering—I thought I knew it all before, but for some reason the message started to sink in. If anything felt out of place in my wardrobe, if I was keeping it because I associated it with a happy memory but it didn't really fit any more, or if I didn't really like it enough to wear it but felt bad because I hadn't worn it enough, it had to go. Keeping it was wasteful. Giving it to a charity shop so it had the opportunity of a second life was the only smart thing to do. Reselling clothes is a pain in the arse, but once you get into it, it's addictive. Essentially, you're giving something to a good home, when you can't look after it any more!

I think that before, I used to see stuff I loved, panic because it was too expensive and might not go with the rest of my clothes, and end up buying something less nice, as a compromise. My wardrobe was full of compromises. Now I know that I'm not stuck with something forever, I trust myself to take risks —but weirdly, I want to give a lot less away because I'm buying what I want. And magically, my new clothes work with everything else I own as I'm wearing stuff that makes me happy!

A couple of years ago, I bought a golden jumpsuit. It's long, strappy and stretchy, loose and low cut. I saw it on the hanger and immediately imagined Bianca Jagger circa 1978 wearing it to climb up the steps of a private jet straight after a wild night at Studio 54. It was fabulous, and fierce, and about as useful and relevant to my life as an economy sized bottle of moat cleaner. So I bought it. I had every intention of returning it, unworn, in a week or so, having grown up and seen sense, but I kept it and wore it on New Year's Eve. Then at a festival.

Then at my hen do. It helps that it's incredibly comfortable, and it does make me look a little bit like a big gold baby—but it also makes me feel joyful and subversive, and truly comfortable in my skin. When I wear it, I feel completely removed from the woman I once thought I ought to be, and at one with the woman I have dreamed of being. I don't think it's especially flattering. When I wear it, I am unignorable. I have superpowers—and all superheroes are at their best when they wear an all-in-one. I took a sartorial risk, and it changed my mood and wardrobe for the better.

The gold jumpsuit has turned into a surprising staple.

When I've made fashion mistakes and spent too much money on stuff I didn't like and couldn't wear, it's rarely been something that is usually considered dramatic and difficult to pull off. It's the white shirts and black trousers, the flattering denim, the muted cashmere and sensible leather handbags. I once wasted a hundred pounds and half an hour staring at my bottom after buying jeans that promised to "radically re-shape" it. I hoped to look as though I had tennis balls in the back pockets, but the effect was more like having shuttlecocks stuck to my thighs. For ages, I wondered what was wrong with my body before deciding, just before the twenty-eight-day return period expired, that there was something wrong with the jeans. I'm embarrassed to admit exactly how many grey jumpers I own, but the only one I wear with any regularity has the words "ALL THE FUN OF THE FAIR" spelled out on the front in neon pink sequins.

I don't have an immaculate capsule wardrobe. I still spend hours each week standing in front of my clothes wondering why I have four yellow sundresses and one wearable pair of jeans. Occasionally, I buy a massive straw hat that I'll wear once a year, spending the whole day running after it as it gets blown off my head. But I do have a growing sense of the sort of woman I am, and what that woman wants to look like. I'm starting to realize that I can't dress for anyone but myself, and I need to be kind to myself in order to make the best choices. Otherwise I really wouldn't have anything to wear, and that's not a problem I can afford to have if I wish to survive the next British winter.

Your LBB
A little black book of really helpful style advice

Everyone knows about eBay being a brilliant space to buy and sell your stuff—but if you love high fashion and can't afford to buy new, French site Vestiare Collective is a treasure trove of beautiful second-hand bits and pieces. It's also a great place to sell your stuff to appreciative potential buyers.

If for any reason it's too difficult to get to the charity shop, it's worth checking if the charity will come to you. Arrange collections either by phone or via the website.

The app Lyst allows you to curate a list of all your favorite shops, brands and designers, points you in the direction of new stuff you might like and, crucially, lets you know when something you adore goes on sale. Shop Style is like Google for clothes. If you've been dreaming of a silver jacket, put the term in the search box and it will find you every single silver jacket that is available for sale on the internet.

Instead of envying your style crushes, take a screenshot of the picture and put it on a Pinterest board. You'll build up a portable scrapbook of the looks you love, and you can see your style evolve. It's very useful when you're out shopping.

Always go with your gut. Never buy anything you don't feel quite right in, just because a friend loves it—and if you adore your look, you don't need a second opinion.

A Few Words About...

The Internet

Try to tell anyone under thirty how to use the internet and it's a bit like telling a Labrador how to eat its dinner. We're one of the first generations to grow up online, and we're really just getting to grips with how not to use the internet. Most of us are tech savvy and excited about trying and embracing every new device. We buy apps to help us sleep, and devices to make us run. If we want to learn how to make a chicken casserole, we'll watch a video online. We might get stuck in a four-hour YouTube loop, and emerge blinking, hungry, and unable to remember what we meant to do before we got distracted by a compilation of TV theme tunes. Effectively, if life throws us any kind of challenge or asks us any sort of question, if we were born after 1980, we'll Google it first. I have Googled "little sister's middle name?" before. That is how lazy and stupid the internet has made me.

It's as good and bad as the billions of people who use it.

It keeps us connected. It's full of ideas, art, gossip, facts, stories, opinions, beauty, and cruelty. You can use the internet to read the complete works of the Brontë sisters in their entirety—and on the same computer, on the same day, find a video of a man having sex with a horse. It makes me think of Patrick Kavanagh's poem

"Advent"—"Through a chink too wide, there comes in no wonder." We can see everything all at once, but what does that leave us to dream about? Can we remember how to work out anything for ourselves, when we've grown up trusting a machine to tell us what to eat and how to get home?

I started to use the internet before I reached my teens. It was sold to me as a soulless, virtual, electronic system, as functional as plumbing, and with slightly less emotional resonance, but it has brought me so much real, human joy and pain. Most of us discovered it at the same time as our parents, and if there was a technological problem, the grown-ups would call upon us to fix it. But, it causes other problems, too, and the adults who would usually guide us through them were stumped—they understood it less than we did. We've had no map or any kind of guidance, and we've had to trust our instincts, and sometimes deal with the consequences when they lead us astray. It's an endless, beautiful, brutal forest. We're all by ourselves, hunting for the good berries and hiding from wolves.

The internet is full of spaces for us to share ourselves with the world. We're encouraged to be open, and tell our stories without boundaries—but we're constantly told, in the same breath, that it isn't safe and that we need to shut ourselves down and stop giving our secrets away. Some days I find the internet enormously comforting. When I'm sad and scared about something, I can usually find some words written by someone who has felt the same way.

However, if I'm feeling slightly insecure about my career, my body or my ability to make ghost-shaped meringues at Halloween, I can go from zero to shitty in less than three clicks. I grew up knowing how to use the internet, but it's only in the last couple of years that I've realized it's important to use it as a life-enhancing force for good, and that if I binge on it and don't use it mindfully, it can make me fearful and anxious, as well as exacerbating my tendency to compare myself with absolutely everyone in the universe and come to the conclusion that they are clever, perfect, beautiful gods and models, and I have the aesthetic and intellectual value of day-old poo in a carrier bag. If your confidence and self-esteem are even slightly wobbly, the internet can be like cocaine for your self-loathing levels.

Here is my personal internet search history, which is now twenty years old:

It's a hot, bright June morning in 1996. I'm sitting in the assembly hall. There's a lingering scent of sandwiches, synthetic cinnamon and ferocious BO, as half of us have reached the point of physical maturity when deodorant becomes a necessity, and a quarter of us mistakenly believe that Impulse body spray is as effective as Sure or Mitchum. Some of us are talking about the previous evening's *Newsround*, which had a feature about a new group called the Spice Girls, set to be "this summer's pop phenomenon". The headmaster shushes us, because he has a very important, exciting announcement. The rumors are true. The school is getting the internet! We will be able to "surf" (here he makes quotation marks with his fingers) the World Wide Web in the library, for fifteen minutes at a time at lunch, if we sign up on the noticeboard opposite the art room, as long as he can persuade a dinner lady to supervise us. The hall is abuzz.

"I don't think I'm an internet sort of person, really," I say to my friend Megan, who is sitting next to me. "I think I'll leave it."

"We don't need it, do we?" she replies. "I mean, we have Encarta!"

It's June again, and we're in the year 2000. The future has arrived, and even my tech-resistant, frightened family are on the internet! Mum and Dad have limited us to half an hour a day, but that's fine because we can use it at school in our lunch breaks. I'm in love. Every day I sneak into the computer room before lessons, log into a Yahoo account and write a thousand words about how I've never felt this way before, how kissing him is "like drinking fine wine" (and at this point in my life, my exposure to wine is limited to the odd glass of Jacob's Creek Merlot with my Sunday lunch), how I can't get to sleep at night because I can't stop thinking about him. Of course, I've never felt this way before—I'm fifteen! I've really experienced just three other feelings—sleepy, grumpy, and hungry. Sometimes the internet is "down" and I weep because I think it means our love is doomed. We are Romeo and Juliet. Our families conspire to keep us apart. They don't understand that we can be so young and so passionate. Why else would they be so cruel as to take us on fortnight-long holidays, timed to separate us for a whole month? Or brandish a BT bill and tell us that they don't go to work in order to pay for us to chat for three hours at a time on MSN Messenger? We should run away together. It's the only way our love can survive! And if we left home, we could always use the internet at the library.

It's the autumn of 2004. I'm a fresher at the University of Leeds. My parents (the cruel ones who wouldn't let me talk to my boyfriend on the internet for twenty-four hours a day) have bought me a laptop. An enormous sum of money appears in my bank account, a loan from the government, and I spend £70 of it to pay for a year of internet access. Then I discover eBay. By late November, I can barely afford to feed myself but I have a great collection of fancy French skincare and "authentic" Dior sunglasses.

Come the summer of 2006, once again a new, technological arrival is the source of gossip and great excitement. (Happily, my new friends and I now have a stronger grasp on the concept of personal hygiene.) Facebook is coming to Leeds! People who know people at Oxford, Cambridge, Bath, and Warwick have been talking about this online

friend directory for some time. I'm skeptical, after struggling to person-
alize a MySpace page. I sign up and see.

It's still summer 2006 and I'm logged onto Facebook every day. I look
at it when I wake up, and then dash back from the bathroom to see if
any exciting, new-friend requests have arrived while I was in the shower. Everyone else seems more popular than I am, everyone has more
pictures than I have, and the longer I look, the harder it is to feel good
about myself afterwards. But I can't stop. I begin to regret taking a gap
year. If only Facebook had arrived after I'd done my final exam!

In the summer of 2009, I sign up for Twitter. It seems stupid—just roll-
ing Facebook status updates with no further function.

Why do we need that? But I work for a magazine, and my editor
says it's handy to keep an eye on what celebs and their handlers are
talking about. I mention it to the men I message and meet for dates on
Soulmates, Match, and MSF. They can't see it taking off either.

By the summer of 2010, I'm finally over my Facebook addiction. I'm
checking Twitter every twenty minutes.

In October 2010, I get my first iPhone.

In November 2010, I leave it under a table at a restaurant.

The iPhone is retrieved, and it's almost impossible to lose it again
because it's never not in my hand. I take pictures, I read the news, I look
at train times, I make my voice sound like T-Pain's—but mostly I'm
locked in a cycle of Twitter, Facebook, Twitter, email, Facebook, email.
Sometimes it has good news for me, and sometimes something negative,
hurtful or upsetting. I'm constantly touching and scrolling, hoping for
the hit of recognition or validation that will keep me going until the

next one. I leave my job to start a freelance career, and this legitimizes my obsessive addiction. "I need to check my email! It might be work!" I scream over dinner, and sometimes it is. Anyone can reach me at any point, and I think it's reasonable for them to expect me to respond to all requests immediately, because email is urgent.

In February 2012, someone shares a funny piece of writing on Twitter, and it makes me laugh so hard that I feel compelled to find the author and tell him how much I loved it. We tentatively retweet each other's jokes and *Simpsons* references. We meet up and go for a drink on the day after my birthday.

By July 2012 I am ready to go on holiday with my Twitter boyfriend. I learn that I am capable of getting a commission from an editor on email and writing the feature on my phone while I wait in the airport security line. I spend the duration of a flight to New York thinking obsessive thoughts about whether the editor received my email, whether my work was good enough and whether she might be furious with me for failing to respond while I'm up in the air.

In the summer of 2015, I write a piece for the *Guardian* about the problems of being a woman using public transport, the strange men that harass and frighten us on buses and trains and the sad fact that, for the sake of our safety, we have to smile and be civil. We can't usually scream at them, or even scream for help. Thousands of people read it, share it and get in touch with me to tell me it comforted them, and that they were glad I wrote it. Hundreds of people read it and get in touch to tell me I'm stupid, delusional, a fat cow who should think herself lucky to have her butt pinched on a crowded train, because they wouldn't touch me with a toilet brush, women don't have a right to move around freely and safely, and I should shut up. A well-known, right-wing, middle-aged commenter gets a whole, cruel column out of it, writing an 800-word personal attack, which is published in a magazine that my nearly ninety-year-old granny reads.

Every time I pick up my phone, I see a notification telling me that someone has shared the hateful video, someone thinks I'm ugly, someone wants to rape me, someone thinks I'm wholly un-rapeable. I lock my Twitter account so that no one else can follow me. I write about what's happening. An existing follower tells me to "just ignore it". I feel sick and stupid and I want to cry. It's just words. I don't have to look at them, but I can't stop thinking about these waves of hate crashing into my account, the idea that strangers have these thoughts about me, let alone feel the need to write them down. My phone is a bomb. This tiny, overpriced device, the thing I use to speak to my mum and tell my boyfriend I love him and send my friends birthday wishes and directions and pictures of seal pups, has become a vessel for people who don't know me but hate me. People who want to make me cry and feel scared.

My boyfriend takes me away to the seaside, and we swim in a warm hotel pool and order room-service spaghetti Bolognese. We go to a gallery and look at pictures of lobsters, and in a second-hand book shop, I find a copy of *Valley of the Dolls*, which I love and have already read many times, but I keep lending it to people and not getting it back. Defiantly, I tweet that I am having a lovely time, and talk about the pleasures of rereading beloved books. One of my editors messages me to ask, "Will you write about that for us?" I feel good. I am a person in the world with a voice, and I want to make myself heard. I can go online, and be listened to.

It's a misty morning in October 2015, and in a few hours I shall be marrying that man I met on Twitter. I'm so excited that I share this news the only way I know how—in less than 140 characters. Friends and strangers shower me with love and good wishes. Not one person is mean about how I managed to get someone to marry me, or how fat I might look in a wedding dress.

Twenty hours later, I lie on top of the bedclothes with my new husband, our fingertips touching, as we hold our phones and search Facebook and Instagram for pictures—for proof that the crazy, lovely, magical day that we just spent together actually happened.

We can, and do, blame the internet for every terrible thing that happens to us. Social media especially seems to have reached a tipping point, where everything posted is mean, people criticize before they praise and everyone furiously defends their right to an opinion—even though that opinion is usually about how everyone and everything else is terrible, toxic, morally bankrupt and probably racist. We're all angry. We take that anger online, and it multiplies. Social media isn't a space that lends itself to considered, nuanced thought. We can type faster than we think, piling vile insults and violent threats on top of each other until we've created a landscape that looks like a Hogarth painting in binary code.

It has to be said that it's rarely twenty-somethings that cause the most problems. Often, the people who haven't grown up online are the ones who don't seem to grasp the power that the internet has, and the amount of upset it can bring. They've never had to censor themselves in any other space, and sometimes they don't seem to understand that while a thoughtless spoken insult can fade into the air, a snide post on a Facebook wall remains etched on our memories, and the servers, forever.

A couple of years ago, I was involved in a workshop for a contemporary ballet about teens and social media. I was there to help with writing the storyboard, and I'd get together with the dancers and choreographer to discuss the research that had been gathered after talking to teens at schools and colleges, about how they used the internet and how it made them feel.

My favorite story involved a young girl who was spotted by her next-door neighbor as she was buying a sausage roll from a bakery just after 6 p.m. The neighbor yelled, "Don't sell that girl a sausage roll, her mum's about to give her some tea!" The girl went home and told her mum what had happened, and instead of thanking the neighbor, or just speaking to her about it over the fence, she went straight to Facebook to post, "So, you think you can tell my kids what they can and can't eat?" tagging the neighbor and adding a bright red, frowny emoji. The neighbor retaliated. The mum answered back, and what should have been a small, silly, quickly forgotten dispute became a digital war that lasted for months. The whole street became involved. Distant relatives from Australia would chime in overnight, triggering new levels of hostility. The daughter disabled her own Facebook account because she felt so stressed and embarrassed by the whole, horrendous drama.

The sausage roll may have been the bullet that began the war, but the story is a real cautionary tale about social media and poor impulse control. It's strangely comforting. I like to think that the majority of internet negativity comes from people who are relatively new to it, who struggle to understand the impact that their words can have, and don't fully grasp that hiding behind a screen might feel dehumanizing but the people who feel the force of the words are made from flesh and blood.

We often pay attention to the angriest voices because they shout the loudest, but I hope that it's only a matter of time before those lone forces of fury figure out what the rest of us already know—if you wouldn't run into a café and scream into strangers' faces that you don't like their outfit or their decision to put milk in their coffee, you really, really don't need to say anything similar online.

I think there's a chance that the internet will eventually make us nicer and more accountable. We're at our bitchiest and cruelest when we don't think the subject will hear us—but everything we say online is said out loud. It will take a while, but social media might be the thing that teaches us to think before we speak, and to save our most wicked observations for when we're among close friends, rather than being mindlessly and automatically negative. However, for now it's turned us all into teenagers. Ironically, the younger you are, the easier it is to get through internet puberty. When you're still growing up and getting older and wiser, you're going to be bringing that newfound maturity online.

Do you really need to tweet that?
A handy guide

Are you being mean to, or about, anyone? It doesn't matter if it's a friend of a friend, a famous celebrity with 50 bajillion followers, or an anonymous egg who has important penis pictures that must be DM'd to you urgently. No matter how great the temptation is, don't be mean. Block, mute, privately message a good friend and share your opinion with them, write down all of your bitchy thoughts on a piece of paper and burn it. But if it isn't kind, if it isn't supportive, if you could imagine it upsetting your mum if it got read out on the news, delete, delete, delete.

Are you giving advice? Did anyone ask you for it? Unsolicited advice is usually about as welcome and useful as the body polishers that come with the big toiletry gift boxes that are only ever given as emergency Christmas presents.

Occasionally, someone will ask a question and you will have the answer. You don't need to hit reply if you just have an answer. If someone says they're looking for a nice pub near Primrose Hill, do not say, "London's rubbish, my favorite pub is in the New Forest." If an internet friend is asking advice about getting a puppy, it's not the right time to tell them that, personally, you prefer kittens.

Asking a question? Could you just Google it? Google it.

Never say, "Off to New York! Any tips?" when you really mean "ZOMG you guys! The Big Apple! So excited! I am going to the magic land of Friends and Annies, both Hall and Little Orphan, and Bloomingdale's and bagels and Billy on the Street and I couldn't be giddier if I was eight years old and Mickey Mouse was meeting me at the airport! But I desperately want to sound cool and casual about this, so everyone thinks I'm a legit, martini-drinking grown-up."

Never respond to anyone's "Going to New York!" shout-out by recommending Central Park, the Empire State Building, or the Magnolia Bakery; or by telling them to go to California instead.

Don't be afraid to tell people that you love their work, they've made you smile, you were just having a conversation with someone else about how great they are, or you thought they might enjoy a picture of a bear cub having a bath, attached.

If you see a friend being savaged by a horrible troll, send a private message of love and support. Resist the temptation to jump in and attack the troll, or you will still be going at it by teatime. This sorry business once led to me dropping my phone in the bath, and I can't even remember who it was I was going in to bat for. If a stranger picks a vicious fight with you or someone you love, they are an irredeemable dick. Nothing you say is going to make them back off, murmuring, "Oh, no, sorry, I was wrong!"

If booze makes you horny or belligerent, don't tweet drunk, but if you're full of whisky warmth and *joie de vivre*, no one will begrudge you the odd, tipsy, "In a taxi, the streetlights make the trees look like they're filled with glow-worms. LOVING LIFE!!!" When my feed is full of people being sober, angry, and miserable, I'm always excited to see that someone is loving life.

When a high-profile figure is being discussed, that person does not need to be dragged into the conversation. Should someone say, "Urghh, Kermit the Frog is on TV. again, how does he get work?!?" it is not appropriate to respond with, "I can't believe you're being horrible about @KermitTheFrog! I LOVE @KermitTheFrog!" Now the original tweeter is dobbed in, and your fan enthusiasm has only made your idol aware that some stranger hates him.

Don't go out of your way to correct someone's mistakes. Sometimes Twitter presents us with a choice to be right, or to be kind. Always choose to be kind. If you have an irresistible urge to shout at strangers and tell them how wrong they are, just watch repeats of *Jeopardy!* in order to capture that smug, superior feeling.

Remember, you are not the news. You are using exactly the same internet as everyone else. There are people out there who will get themselves confused with the BBC and grandly announce, "BREAKING: Queen buys new hat." Unless you've actually spotted Her Maj in John Lewis, and you're watching her pick out a trilby while you hide in the back by the tights, it's safe to assume that Reuters has a few people covering any major international developments, and your followers still prefer to be alerted by traditional journalists.

Say sorry. Lots. Your *mea culpa* should runneth over. You're a human being talking to other human beings, and you're all going to be irrational and angry and excited and happy and late and lazy, at each other, all at once. Mistakes will be made. Sometimes we all say the wrong things, or the right thing gets read the wrong way. If you can identify your errors, be sincere about wanting to rectify them and allow yourself to be corrected with good grace, the internet will help you to grow into a great person, as well as being the perfect place to look for heavily discounted train tickets.

CHAPTER NINE

How To Have Sex

I think having sex in the twenty-first century can be more bewildering and complicated than untangling a whole drawer full of broken headphones.

In a way, we've never had it so good. We have theoretical access to a wide range of contraception and vibrators that are charged through USB ports. We have "women friendly" porn and a society that should be progressing, growing up, and becoming increasingly tolerant of everything on the sexual spectrum. *And* we have a wide range of affordable, washable, high-quality bed linen. Hooray!

On the other hand, there's problematic porn, the rise in rape and sexual assault statistics, news stories about young people being humiliated as a result of sexting incidents, super gonorrhea, statistical evidence that we're having less sex because we won't get off Netflix and the fact that a fifth of us currently live with our parents until we're at least twenty-six and still have to sneak upstairs to give silent hand jobs while everyone else is watching a repeat of *The Big Bang Theory*.

The way we think about sex affects everything we do, and similarly, sex is affected by everything—confidence, the way we feel about our bodies, how we relax, what we worry about. So, the good news is that everything you do to feel happier and more comfortable in yourself is great for your sex life, even if the only person that you're having sex with right now is you. (When I say right now, I recommend that you finish the chapter before you start seeing to yourself—but I'm not judging.) Sex itself is supposed to make you feel amazing—not guilty, or fat, or sad, or anxious or uncomfortable. However, it's only because I've experienced all of those feelings, post or mid coitus, that I know that no woman should ever have to put up with it.

In 2013, the Office of National Statistics released results of a study that showed almost one in five women in England and Wales have reported experiencing some form of sexual assault after they turned sixteen. I'm one of them. I was raped by my boyfriend when I was seventeen—and it took me a long time to identify the experience, even though I said, "No," loud and clear, before and during. I talk about my rape openly because I can. Now, I have enough distance to share the experience, and I want to tell the world that I am one of millions of women who have been through this. It isn't our fault. It won't ruin our lives.

What I struggle to describe is the countless experiences I've had since then when I feel as though I haven't been in control, when I woke up drunk in the middle of something I couldn't remember saying yes to, when I've been in bars and on buses and a stranger has touched me when I didn't give them permission to do so. How can we say yes to sex when most of us will meet at least one person who, one way or another, won't listen for an answer?

Some days, I find it really hard to be positive about sex because so many people seem to want to take it from us. Sex is constantly hitting the headlines, but it's never good news. We don't talk about tenderness, or sensuousness, or the joy of desire. We don't celebrate women who love sex and have it on their own terms. The media will call a girl a slut before they'll call a boy a rapist, and this is the cultural problem that's killing our sex lives. When so many of us have an experience that makes us stay silent and feel ashamed, how can we possibly get our bodies back?

It can be done. Here's how I learned to love sex again after serious assault.

Firstly, I did not have a positive relationship with my body at the beginning. It wasn't a good home for me; it wasn't a safe space to live. As I've mentioned, I was bullied extensively at school because I was "fat". Now I know that if I hadn't been just a slightly chubby little girl, the bullies would have probably picked on me for being tall, or wearing a purple coat—"fat" is just an easy term of abuse for the terminally lazy. However, bullies are smart about covering their tracks, and when I complained, there would be a furious argument between my parents and the teachers. So, I shut up. Aged five, I started sacrificing my body to keep the peace, because it didn't seem that important. I didn't seem that important.

The bullies sometimes pulled my skirt up over my head in order to see my "fat-girl pants", so when an elderly man, who had volunteered to babysit, also demanded to see my underwear, I accepted it as another sad element of a fat girl's fate. Now I know that, tragically, millions of children experience sexual abuse, and abusers, like bullies, are experts at manipulating everyone around them to get what they want.

But, back then, I had no idea, and I stayed silent and sad. I'd learned to associate sex with shame before I even understood what sex was, and I often wonder how many other women grew up feeling the same way.

Puberty came early, and that felt like the cruelest joke of all. Strange men stared at my strangely adult breasts, and I felt just as humiliated and horribly self-conscious as I had in the playground. Every lecherous glance was another bully punching me on the bus. I've described my experiences with anorexia and how they damaged my relationship with my body. I binged and purged and spent my early teens becoming dangerously thin.

My body had betrayed me, over and over again—finally, I was its bastard boss. Then I met a boy and fell in love the way that is only possible when you're fifteen, and your bloodstream runs rainbows and Hershey's Kisses. My angles softened. I stopped feeling so scared. When he looked at me, I felt magical for the first time in forever—I felt as happy in my body as I had before I started school, when my mum made me a fairy dress and I wore it every day.

Then one June afternoon I said no, and he didn't listen.

We'd had sex before—I'd lost my virginity to him six months before it happened. Yet it had always been a compromise, with him making me feel as though I was doing him a favor—a favor I'd owed him for a while. My parents had made it very clear that they did not want their Catholic daughter to sleep with anyone before marriage, and all the language they used around premarital sex was colored with mud—it was a dirty deed for a dirty girl. My body was a battleground, parents and boyfriend maintaining separate trenches, leaving me without a settlement to call my own. And then my boyfriend took it, and I realized it was crazy of me to care. It had caused me nothing but problems, and I was happy to abandon it like a burned-out car.

Eventually, we broke up, and I spent the next few years selling myself out to the highest bidder. You like it? It's yours! I don't care for it much myself. I took a death by a thousand papercuts approach of bad sex, worse diets, hurty bras, and a disdain for vitamins. One of the reasons that I spent most of my twenties too frightened to register with a doctor was that, because I was secretly so convinced everything about me was too toxic and rotten to cure, I was equally convinced that I'd step into the doctor's office, be looked up and down and thrown out. "You have all the incurable diseases. Now get out, before you frighten the nice patients."

It's very hard to have a sane, happy sex life when you treat your own body like an albatross. I slept with everyone whom I thought might fix me, or find some good in me—but I was too lost to listen to anyone who might have had an answer.

Then along came the great love of my life. Feminism.

It was a low, slow, rumble of dissent that became constant and unignorable, like the bass line of a monster EDM hit that you hear in a taxi from the airport and then daily for the rest of the summer. I was working at a magazine for teenaged girls and thinking a lot about the life I wanted for them, for my little sisters, for all that these young women were going to be. I was thinking about how my central sexual message—have sex for you, on your terms, when you are ready—was at odds with what I was actually practicing. I was telling everyone that loving your body was important when I was meaner about mine than you might be about a roommate's milk-finishing houseguest. At the same time, I was having conversations with other single women about porn, the people we were dating and how sometimes sex with new people felt less like a collaboration than a negotiation. I fell in with the feminists, and figured out how to live in my body again, and build a home in it.

Through feminism, I started my own sexual revolution. I took off my fat-girl knickers, figuratively and literally. I realized you had to love your body in order to make love with it. After a lifetime of being angry and dismissive, it was time to be tender and kind.

It took a little while. I'm still working on it, and making mistakes, but everything changed when I discovered that sex was bound up with my body. I could either pretend not to see myself or feel myself, to search out the sort of physical contact that would burn the hurt and humiliation away—or I could choose to stop trying to destroy myself, and to rebuild my house instead of trying to burn it down.

So, what about the activity that is supposed to form part of our "typical twenties"—sex with people we don't know terribly well. Sometimes, meaningless sex is just that—an act of intimacy that doesn't need to have further consequences. It doesn't make anyone bad, or difficult, or without value. It's being caught up in a moment of physical joy that doesn't necessarily have any bearing on the rest of your life. Essentially, all that matters is that it makes you feel good. If it doesn't make you happy, it isn't meaningless—it has a bad meaning, and you should avoid it. Unfortunately, it's often hard to know what the outcome will be until you're in bed afterwards, possibly with a non-metaphorical cigar.

I spent half my twenties in long-term, monogamous relationships, and the other half being studly or slutty, depending on the people I'm talking to and their prejudices and preferences. Sometimes I had tender, intense, shudderingly awesome sex with people I didn't know terribly well and sometimes I had awkward, chafing, self-conscious sex with people whom I hoped would validate me. The best sex always happened when I stopped worrying about defining myself, and managed to forget myself. When I felt sexy, beautiful and powerful, I stopped waiting for someone to bestow those qualities on me with their penis.

When I've been single, I've defined myself by my promiscuity. At the start of my twenties I rolled around town like a representative of the Monster Raving Loony Sex Party, only just stopping short of wearing a special "SEX!" hat shaped like an erection, and a T-shirt shouting "Ask me about my hot, horny adventures!" I used to stagger into rooms, one palm pressed into the small of my back, legs splayed like I was about to fall down on an ice rink, shouting, "Girls! You would not believe the night I had! I got well naked with this top lad! Man, I've had some orgasms! Don't you love being a liberated woman?! That burning sensation I get when I pee is a small price to pay for this fabulous, no-strings hook up!"

The fact that I have any friends left from this era of my life is a total mystery.

I think I'd confused sex with the stories I wanted to tell. I was doing what I thought I ought to be doing, without thinking about whether I really desired it. When I came out of my first long-term relationship, I put myself under a lot of pressure to make up for lost time. I assumed that everyone else was having crazy, exotic sex with an array of gorgeous partners, and thought I was deeply pathetic for being monogamous throughout my teens and twenties.

Let's break this down. No one told me that they thought I needed to get my shag on. There was no real element of peer pressure, no conversations when a friend sat me down and said, "You seem uptight. How about sex with a stranger?" I just assumed that other people were judging me, based on my own shitty self-image. I'd seen *Sex And The City*, and in the early Oughts, nobody wanted to be Charlotte. Who was the opposite of Charlotte? Sexy Samantha!

I can picture my past self, "enjoying" my first one-night stand at the age of twenty-one, and I want to say, "Oh, little Daisy, nooooo! Flirt, drink, touch his knee! Kiss until your face is sore! But don't take this mediocre man home with you! It's too much hassle!"

He was a US exchange student, who had come from a campus in South Carolina. Or possibly Chicago. We met in a bar, through a mutual friend. All I remember is being overwhelmed by the sensation that he a) liked me, and b) was American. American! I had never flirted with an American before! I was Judy Garland, getting picked up by a GI! I was Cindy Crawford! If nothing else, it was a ringing endorsement for the quality of my teeth! I felt sexy, special and quite unlike myself, so I asked if he wanted to go back to my place.

It started to go badly when he went to get himself a glass of water from the kitchen and noticed that the sink was so full of dirty dishes that there wasn't enough space to get a glass under the tap, and that I had drawn a big, passive–aggressive cartoon and stuck it to the window. The cartoon featured a plague of giant ants with homicidal tendencies, and the story implied that if my housemates did not do their washing up soon, the ants were coming for us. That night, I learned that there's a difference between being quirky and adorable (which usually just involves having bangs and distractingly weird (using terrible art to shame other people into doing their chores).

Under the glow of my Ikea fairy lights, we tentatively undressed each other and did our best to pretend that we weren't on the brink of changing our minds. Even the kissing was clunky, and it had been awesome when we were both half-cut on cocktails. All I remember thinking is, "This has been going on for absolutely ages," and, "It's weird that his underwear is almost knee length. I wonder if that's an American thing."

He left early the next day, and we did a perfunctory number swap. He didn't say, "Wow, thanks for an unforgettable night of passion!" But then the books and magazines had warned me that he wouldn't, so I didn't worry too much. I put on a tight, belted dress and pouted experimentally in the mirror. So, this was how it felt to be grown-up! I waited until lunch and then texted him to see if he fancied a picnic. I may have made a joke about ants. I am still waiting for his reply.

For a long time, I wondered what I'd done wrong. I didn't understand how he could feel one way about me in a bar, and another in bed. I slept with more people, purely to prove to myself that I could hold their attention. I thought about dressing differently, losing weight, saying less and listening more. In dark moments, when I wasn't obnoxiously bragging about all the sex I was having, I was pleading with my friends to tell me how I could improve myself.

At the time it didn't cross my mind that I was becoming boringly obsessed with impressing someone who hadn't impressed me. I'd been unmoved by our encounter, so why should he feel any differently?

The trouble was that I wanted to base my personality on being "good in bed"—a misnomer, as the first rule of "good in bed" is that you're wild and crazy enough to want it any which way but near a pillow. "Make your man melt by doing it up a fir tree!" is the sort of advice that is accepted, unquestioned, by those of us who aspire to an unattainable universal standard of sexiness.

I think that if you learn nothing else as a sexually active adult, the greatest lesson to take home is that "good in bed" is bullshit.

By my mid-twenties, I'd turned into the sex version of the creepy man in his late thirties who haunts student nights in clubs with semi-functional, light-up dance floors. I had "moves". I'd panic if I started having too much fun, and I'd get caught in a moment only to think, "Oh no! I haven't done that thing with my tongue!" You know that creeping sensation of dread you get at weddings, when the disco starts and the DJ plays "Saturday Night", and after two minutes you realize that you alone have been doing the Macarena? That was my sex life.

This affected my relationships. Sometimes the person I was with got mad because I started to feel tired and lazy, and stopped performing like a pony at an unlicensed Disney ice show. Sometimes sex was the only part of the partnership that worked. When I was in a disastrous relationship with someone who manipulated me and made me feel insecure, the sex seemed amazing because it was the only time when I felt sure of him, and confident that I had his attention. And then I met my husband.

At the start of my twenties, I would have been horrified if Future Me had paid a visit and earnestly explained that I would have the best sex ever with the love of my life. How boring!

How off brand! Also, I'd had enough long-term boyfriends to know that you can't pretend to be enticing and exciting for twenty-four hours a day, with the person you see the most. For a long time, I believed that it was game over for thrilling sexy times just as soon as the other person found out that you sometimes had periods and poops.

But, late in the day, I discovered that sex is magical when you stop thinking and start feeling. When you feel completely comfortable with someone, and sure that they're not going to leave you if they hear you farting or see you in unflattering track pants, you can truly feel comfortable with them. I used to approach sex as though I was a *Bachelor* contestant hoping to get a job on Broadway when the series finished. I moved as though I was expecting someone to hold up score cards at the end.

Now, if I'm honest, I think I'd be lucky to get 10/40 for form and timing, but I'm having too nice a time to care.

I don't think I could have reached this point without experiencing a promiscuous past. For me, sometimes sex has been bad, sad or mad, brilliant and bewildering, desire fueled and desperately dull. Being in a happy, healthy relationship is very good for one's sex life, but in order to get there, I had to try, fail and make mistakes. My husband didn't fix me, or undo my bad decisions. He made me feel comfortable and confident, but ultimately, he just showed me that he wanted to be with the person I had become—not the nervous, sexy show-off who simply couldn't get enough attention or validation to fill herself up.

I haven't given up on skills and trickery, but I don't feel the same anxious need to employ them. I can be wielding a paddle, or tied up in ribbons, wearing a top hat or a tiara or nothing but a towel and a smile. I can be covered in Nutella, or dressed in pleather, but as long as we're together and as long as it's us, us, us in the dark, with the lights on, down an alley, up against a wall or in any bed, in our bed, that's what I want. It's the only non-negotiable.

When you're in a serious, long-term relationship, you make sexual decisions together. I think that you have to accept that sexual intimacy is in a constant state of flux. When it's good, it's very, very good, but you might get sick. You might struggle to do what came easily at the start, and stay committed to each other. You might both get jobs that mean getting up at 5 a.m. and working for fourteen hours, and feel as though you're capable of nothing more arousing than giving each other a light pat on the elbow. Part of growing up is accepting that you'll never be a master of sex—you just need to make sure you feel good, physically and emotionally, and that if you have a partner, they do too. You can get to that point via any route, with any number of people, as long as you're honest with the people you're sleeping with, and most importantly, honest with yourself about what you want.

Five sex lessons I would go back in time to give my twenty-something self

Only ever have sex for love. You don't have to love the other person, but you do have to go in filled with love for yourself.

Never sleep with someone if you don't think you can say his name in the middle without cracking up. (I know this from experience. Sorry, Ken.)

When vibrator shopping, go for something quiet, unless you want your housemates rushing in and telling you to pick up your phone when you're, ahem, ringing your bell.

If anyone in the equation is sleeping with other people and/or hasn't been checked out recently, please use a condom.

There is no such thing as safe sex, only safer sex. And get checked at the clinic regularly, while remembering that everyone there is lovely and professional and no one is judging you.

Do not worry if a visit to the clinic makes you so frantic with worry that you burst into tears and drop snot all over the doctor as soon as your name is called. We've all been there. (And it's almost always fine.)

A Few Words About...

Wanking

I don't think I ever needed anyone to tell me how to touch myself, but I did need a lot of help

when it came to learning that it was nothing to be ashamed of. Now, I'm not advocating that we start touching ourselves up in the middle of Starbucks in order to "make a statement", but I do think we need to have some bold, revolutionary conversations about getting to know ourselves sexually and working out what feels good for us, before we worry about pleasing other people.

When I worked for *Bliss*, I used to dream about writing the ultimate, unpublishable feature—a masturbation guide for our readers. We'd get so many letters from girls who were so scared of sex. They'd slept with boys, and it had been a total anticlimax in every sense. They wanted to have sex with their boyfriend, but they were haunted by the apocryphal story of their best-friend's cousin, who went to wind band with a girl in the year below who was giving someone a hand job and got pregnant through her pants. They'd sent someone a topless photo, and that person had laughed at their nipples, and they believed they could only find sexual happiness and acceptance if they met someone who was prepared for them to keep their bra on at all times, even in the bath.

I wanted to hug these girls tight, sit them down and say, "Honey. Of course you think sex is scary. It's because you live in this shitty Western world where it's presented as something that is done to you. All you need to do is spend a happy half hour with your hands down your pants, and you'll soon realize that there's no point having sex with someone unless they're loving, and lovely, and kind, because you can have sex with yourself whenever you want, and it's usually much better than having sex with someone who fingers you like they're trying to return their iPhone to its factory settings."

I'm sure the girls who wrote in were doing a fair bit of independent exploration, because I was when I was a teen. I'm also sure that some of them felt weird and embarrassed and disgusting and alone, and that the world would end if anyone ever found out about what they were up to, because I did, too.

Masturbation is a brilliant hobby. It's free. You don't need to worry about STDs. It helps to make your orgasms stronger and longer, and you learn all sorts about the way your body works, and as you get more comfortable yourself, it's easy to look a future partner in the eye and tell him or her, "I really like it when you rub on my clit with your thumb for thirty seconds in an clockwise motion," instead of saying, "Um, yes, on, you know, my, there. NOT THAT THERE!" It helps you sleep. It cures hangovers. It releases stress and tension. If there was a pill that produced half the side effects of a good wank, the pharmaceutical industry would double in value and someone would make a whimsical romantic comedy about it all called *Self-love and Other Drugs*.

So, once you're in your twenties, and in a position to prioritize your sexy self and the pursuit of pleasure, learning how to become a master of your own body is a box worth ticking.

I asked my friend Sam what she does:

Firstly, I can't believe we're having this conversation but yes, I masturbate regularly and I'm a big fan of it. I did it in a covert, ashamed way as a teenager, fell out of the habit when I was in a relationship and then got a vibrator as a joke Secret Santa gift. Curiosity got the better of me and some of the comments I got made me think, "Oh, maybe I'm the only one not doing this." I felt so self-conscious, and then it felt really good, and I started to feel happier and calmer generally—I always slept better after an orgasm. Now I think that it's a part of wellbeing, like exercise and healthy eating!

Another friend, Cara, tells me:

I've never been able to come with a partner or on my own, but I still masturbate a few times a week. I had a massage when I was travelling in Thailand, and the woman doing it told me about the importance of touch, and touching yourself in a loving way. At the time, I wrote it off as hippy nonsense, but in the last couple of years I've really come round to it. I find it so easy to think really negative things about myself, but you can't slag yourself off when you're stroking yourself!

Personally, I think that it's helped my body image hugely. Sometimes I really struggle to feel confident, because I live in a world in which women are valued because of the way they look. I know it isn't fair, but some days it's hard to ignore the negative feelings and not lose miserable hours staring into space and asking the universe why I don't look like Chrissy Teigen (even though I know, deep down, that I would rather look like me and enjoy occasional unrestricted access to a cheeseboard). But when I make myself come, I feel as golden and gleamingly desirable as an Oscar. I feel like a woman who can make her own rocket fuel. The house could fall down and catch fire, and I'm packing so much magic in my underwear that, when I'm caught in the moment, I wouldn't even notice.

Sex, like everything else, is a confidence game, and everything that makes you feel good about yourself and your life is worth pursuing. You must love yourself if you want love to find you, and I'd go further and say that it's imperative to learn to love yourself with your hands if you want to meet someone who is going to push the right buttons.

So where do you start? How do you get in the mood? If you've got a high sex drive, you probably don't need much encouragement, but if you're not revving yourself up regularly, it can be difficult to get in touch with your inner horn. (I'd like to apologize for that pun, but I'm not going to.)

Jessie, who works in merchandising, tells me:

This is embarrassing, but a few years ago, I read 50 Shades of Grey. Everyone I knew was really rude about it and said that they didn't think it was hot at all. I read it, out of curiosity, and that was all the encouragement I needed!

My brain knew it was ridiculous but everything else was saying, "Let's go!" I loved it, but I felt so bad that my source of sexual stimulation was desperately uncool.

In a sexual scenario, anything goes between adults, as long as all parties are consenting enthusiastically. When you touch yourself, two parties are involved—your body and your imagination. Everyone else is banished from the bedroom, shower or sitting-room sofa (perhaps avoid that as a location if you have roommates). You're allowed to be turned on by anything you like. If you can make yourself come by thinking about a three-way with Scooby and Scrappy Doo, that's fine.

Most dramatic fantasies are only a problem when you attempt to translate them into real life. When it's just you, your hands and your head, treat it like a trip to the circus, whip that lion and bring on the dancing girls!

This brings us to porn. If you leave your house, use public transport or go to shops and gyms and salons where the TV is on in the background, it's quite hard not to watch porn. I suspect that most shampoo adverts would be confiscated under the Obscene Materials Act if you took screenshots and posted them to someone who lives in 1951. Sometimes I find it hard to work out where advertising ends and proper porn begins. Admittedly, you don't see actual primary sexual organs on screen in the middle of the day, but no matter what you're looking at, there's a lot of airbrushed flesh, acrylic nails and unconvincing moaning.

Porn can be bad and brilliant. I know that there's a lot of material out there that doesn't promote female pleasure, consent, positive body image or an enlightened approach to interior design. I've seen a lot of soft-bellied, bald men growling, "Do me, baby! You love my massive dick!" at women so perfectly proportioned that they might have been designed by Rodin. Some porn makes sex look like a sad community service. "We'll let you off the speeding fine if you go to traffic school, and pretend to have an orgasm when my friend Terry sticks his finger up your butt. Oh, yeah, sorry, he's been chopping jalapenos."

However, porn can also be an incredibly valuable educational tool, and while there's a long-held belief that it's exploitative, demeaning and bad for body image, there's plenty of positive erotic material available that celebrates a wide range of women, and what they want. Try some strategic Googling (with Safe Search off). Film-maker Erika Lust, who won a feminist porn award for her film *Cabaret Desire* in 2012, is a proponent of ethical porn, and told *GQ Magazine*, "It's for people who have standards and ideas, and value and want the same things from the things they are consuming, whether it's eggs, clothes or porn." Essentially, porn is a product (and it's thought that now one in three viewers are women) and it doesn't really matter what you watch as long as you do plenty of research on how it's made, and ensure that you're not getting off on something that is harming the wider sexual environment.

Remember, "self-love" isn't just a euphemism. When we touch ourselves, we are learning how to be tender with ourselves. I used to think that sexuality was something projected onto me, a force that sprang from the person who was looking at me, something that I could never be in charge of. Masturbation taught me that I can get to know my body better than anyone else, and that's something to be proud of. I like to think that might be why it's called "masturbation"—it makes us masters of our own universe.

Sexy reading list

The great thing about sexy books and written porn is that you know you're paying for something with fewer ethical question marks, and that nobody involved has been coerced into taking part or into doing anything they'd prefer not to be doing, or has been on a shoot that has overrun and they're not being paid properly. If, like Jessie, you read *50 Shades* and you're looking for more stimulus (or you'd like a sexy book but you heard about that famous bit with the ginger and got put off), here are my sexy reading recommendations.

House of Holes, **Nicholson Baker.** Subtitled "A book of raunch", this might be the maddest, most dazzlingly cheerful erotic book I've ever read. Its characters access private fantasy playgrounds through some of the most mundane portals, and the message is about celebrating desire and diversity. Inspiring.

Les Liaisons Dangereuses, **Pierre Choderlos de Laclos.** In common with a lot of eighteenth-century literature, this is hugely problematic in places (and should come with a trigger warning) but I'd say 30 percent of my early sexual fantasies were inspired by the adventures of the Marquise de Merteuil.

The Man Who Made Husbands Jealous, **Jilly Cooper.** As a life-long fan of Cooper, I know some of her men are monsters, but hero Lysander lives to bring happiness and sexual confidence to neglected women. It's lovely.

Valley of the Dolls, Jacqueline Susann
My copy always falls open to the part where sexy starlet Jennifer is being seduced by her friend Maria. She goes to sleep with
quite a few men, but it's nowhere near as hot.

Delta of Venus, Anaïs Nin
This is the perfect "dirty" book, because Nin is a legitimate lit-
erary powerhouse and you don't ever need to feel embarrassed
if a copy falls out of your bag. The prose is beautiful, and while
objectification is never a good thing, it's thrilling to see men's
bodies viewed through horny female eyes.

CHAPTER TEN

How To Relax

Let's start by breathing deeply. Close your eyes. You're wandering through a sun-dappled forest. You can hear the gentle chirp of birds, the buzz and hum of...

OW! OWWWWWWWWW! You've been bitten by a bastard mosquito! OWWW! Sorry about that! Moving on! Ignoring the searing pain and growing sensation of itchiness on your bare shoulder, you walk through the imaginary forest, your sense of calm growing as you experience the fantasy, sense by sense. The warmth of the sun on your back. The silk of a petal between your fingertips. The scent of... urghhhh! What is that? Is that fox poo? Never mind. Just focus on the sun on your back, the sound of snapping bracken and urgent footsteps as a suspicious stranger behind you starts to give chase...

This is what happens whenever I try to relax. I love the idea of chilling out, but I'm not naturally built for it, and I hate that the word is always issued as an instruction, usually when you're really stressed. The people who say, "Just relax!" are the same ones who aren't making sufficient apologies for the fact that they've just locked you out of your apartment or lost the bag that they said they'd keep an eye on while you went to the bathroom. If being told to "calm down" was wise and effective advice, I wouldn't bother writing this, as I'd assume everyone was already in a hammock sipping rum-based cocktails.

Relaxing is just one more thing to worry about, another scary, hard to achieve item on an endless list. Also, I resent that relaxation is presented as a natural activity, and it's somehow associated with recordings of birdsong, Himalayan salt scrubs, wind chimes and blankets woven from grass that died of natural causes—when relaxing is probably the least natural thing we do. It's all about fight or flight! Predators are everywhere! We have evolved to protect the cave, to jump up and scream when a picture falls off a wall because it might be burglars!

Also, we're permitted to relax only when we've done some serious achieving. We can't start off relaxed—we have to put in some serious work, just to be allowed to do it. Good relaxing equals a high-powered businesswoman who earned 10 million dollars during a morning's trading, did some remote project management on the school for disadvantaged children that she is funding, and then ran ten miles. She is allowed a luxurious massage at an expensive spa. Bad relaxing equals The Dude from *The Big Lebowski*. He's just too relaxed! No one wants to entertain the idea that the path to happiness and contentment might lie in smoking weed all day and going bowling in your dressing gown. That said, weed does have the unfortunate effect of triggering anxiety and paranoia. I wonder if any deleted scenes feature The Dude being chased through an imaginary forest...

However, relaxing is a really important skill. It's vital that we sometimes stop what we're doing, or rather, *do* what we're doing. Mentally, I'm often in many different places at once, and not because I'm experimenting with transcendental meditation and visiting thrilling, distant lands of my imagination. I'm crossing a road and reading an email, while my brain skips further ahead to my recycling bin, to my laundry basket, to the weird patch at the back of my fridge, then runs across the offices of London to eavesdrop on the imaginary things my editors and bosses might be saying about me.

This is why we all have those panicked moments when we think, "Did I lock the door today? Did I leave my keys in it?" It's because our heads and our hands are rarely in the same place, and if you're an anxiety sufferer like me, a fellow member of Team Freak Out, your brain will whizz over to your front door and picture it banging open in the breeze to reveal an apartment now empty of all your landlord's furniture, and on fire.

What's weird is that if you were to come home and find you'd been burgled, you'd almost certainly handle it well. You'd be forced to pay attention to what was going on, live in the moment, and focus. When you're facing a crisis, it's at the forefront of your mind, and you'll find you have the skills and resources to do whatever needs to be done. It's unlikely that you'll start worrying about whether or not you remembered to reply to an email.

I'm not advising anyone to get robbed on purpose to see if the theory works. Our heads are full of hypotheticals.

Personally, I waste a huge amount of energy worrying about what might happen, and whether I'll cope. Sometimes it helps me to manage my anxiety, and think about relaxing, if I remember that when I'm worrying the most, I probably have nothing to worry about. I quickly become obsessed with the many things that might go wrong, when the bad thing has yet to happen and may not even happen at all.

I'm not smart enough or wise enough to come to this conclusion on my own. I had to get mugged.

It was late afternoon on a bright, humid summer's day. Life felt new and exciting, but stressful, too. I'd been seeing a new boyfriend for a few months—he turned out to be my future husband, but I did not know that then. I was also five weeks into my freelancing career, and celebrating the fact that I could go and work in coffee shops during the day while worrying about whether I would get enough assignments to be able to buy any coffee.

I had just left my flat, in an unlovely part of south London, and was walking to the subway, down a big, busy road. There were four lanes of traffic, and I was surrounded by people, in cars, waiting for the bus or going to the shop to buy an ice cream. I was staring at my phone and trying to work out how to reply to an email from an editor who wanted me to write twice the number of words we'd previously agreed on, for half the price. Is there a way, I thought despairingly, of saying, "This is totally unfair and I hate you!" without sounding like a whiny bitch? Stress made me exaggerate. Why was I always in these situations? My life was so stressful and horrible! Then, I felt a stranger's hand close around mine. Since I am an idiot, I clung to the phone like it was the one true ring and I was Gollum. The stranger pulled. I clung tighter. He threw me to the ground, and I gashed my knee on the pavement. It started bleeding and I kept screaming as if he was abducting my child and not trying to relieve me of four inches of glass and metal with a maximum resale value of £100.

Eventually, he gave up, and I went to ring the police from a cafe, while brushing bits of asphalt from my sticky knee.

Now, I can't stress this enough. If you ever get mugged, do not hold on to your phone. You don't know what someone else is prepared to do to get it. I was very stupid, and very, very lucky. The experience was traumatic, and it made me deeply anxious about walking alone, especially along that particular road, and about holding any useful or valuable objects in plain sight. The upside was that, for some time, I felt much more relaxed about the problems that worried me. I was able to tell the editor exactly what I needed to tell her, in a short, civil message, because I wasn't stifled by the fear that it might make her hate me. No matter how angry or displeased she felt, she probably wasn't going to mug me. For a couple of weeks, I slept soundly for eight hours a night because my litany of pre-sleep worries and woes was replaced by, "Have I been the victim of any petty crime lately? No! Hurrah! This has been a good day!"

Obviously, any kind of physical attack can be traumatic, and it's not fair to expect anyone to respond to it with gratitude and optimism. It's hardly a present from the universe. However, it brought me perspective when I needed it badly, and made me very aware of everything I had, and how thankful and grateful I was for it—not just my stupid phone, which was eventually stolen from me by a fraudulent *Big Issue* seller in a branch of Pret, six months later. So how can we experience the strangely relaxing effects of a mugging without actually being mugged?

For me, it helped when I realized that "live in the moment!" isn't just annoying unsolicited advice offered by that auntie with tie-dye tendencies after she's opened a second bottle of rosé. It's a basic safety instruction. If I'm worrying about stuff that might happen instead of paying attention to what's going on around me, I'm too distracted to look after myself.

When I started putting my phone away on walks, turning my music off and keeping my eyes out for muggers, I started noticing the good stuff. The streets were lined with trees, dense with porcelain blossom or glossy green leaves. Every other pedestrian had a dog, fluffy, hairy, silly, or serious, and each more adorable than the last. I saw a boy of about five, wearing a T-shirt adorned with a bright red lobster and eating a Cornetto with the same levels of joy and concentration that Anthony Bourdain might have engaged when approaching the tasting menu at El Bulli.

I'm embarrassed by how obvious this sounds, but the simple technique of "paying attention when walking, so you don't get robbed or run over" has turned me into a total hippy, and it's wonderful.

Meditation and mindfulness have both become extremely fashionable, whether you approach them in an immersive "Beatles meeting the Maharishi" sense, or if you just download an app with pre-recorded wind chimes and instructions issued by someone who sounds like their double dose of Night Nurse just kicked in. I've tried the apps, and sometimes I've found them incredibly effective. However, I do wonder whether we're making the practice more complicated than it needs to be. If the idea of spending a lot of time and money on nurturing your innate spirituality appeals to you, there are plenty of outlets for it. But I believe we can feel the benefits, and relax much more quickly, by simply turning off our phones and going for a fifteen-minute walk.

As our minds fill up, it becomes harder and harder to access the part of ourselves that prevents us from mentally overheating and crashing. It's like a muscle, and we must keep it supple with frequent, effective relaxation. I still fall into the trap of thinking that relaxation must be earned, and I'm allowed to do it only if I complete every task on an unending list, and achieve a bonus of six impossible things before breakfast. Slowly, I'm learning that I work, and work well, only if I make relaxation a priority. It's not a treat; it's more like a multivitamin. It's a way of exercising my whole brain, and not just the parts that scream, "DO MORE! DO IT FASTER! DO IT NOW!"

I've found that the best way to quiet the noise in my head is to use my hands. Most of us work in fields that involve constant communication and mental stimulation. We're all made of meetings, spreadsheets, and emails. For the most part, our ancestors didn't do this. They made pots, or jam, or horseshoes. To be fair, the modern office is a much safer and healthier environment than any space in which people were using hot, sharp implements while they relied on candlelight to help them see what they were doing. No one wants to return to the days of lace making, or any other intricate work that would render you blind by your thirty-fifth birthday. But it's much easier to be mindful while you're doing a task that primarily employs a different part of your body. I think we need to be able to escape our minds for a bit in order to manage them, and that's hard to do when almost all we do, personally and professionally, is based on relationships and conversations. Our minds are overused and overstimulated. We've broken the off switch, but we can fix it with our hands.

Embarrassingly, my switch-off tasks are the sort of things you might do if you were a very posh person at a Swiss finishing school in 1928. I cook, I lose myself in dull domestic tasks, and, occasionally, I arrange flowers. If I'm in a very bad way and can't sit still or keep calm, I find something incredibly soothing about doing the washing-up. It's cleansing to fill a sink with hot, soapy water, and comforting to feel my hands swaddled in Marigolds, protected from the sharp heat of the liquid. It's satisfying, in an elemental way, to take something dirty and disordered and make it clean and tidy. My mum claims that ironing has a similar effect. However, no chores are relaxing when you share your house with people who chill out by avoiding bleach and dish soap. It's hard to experience the soothing effects of the task if you're doing the washing-up for three other people. Again. But there's always flower arranging.

My love of flowers is something I discovered by accident. When I was first diagnosed with anxiety, I found that the bad feelings didn't build up so much if I spent a little time every day in a green space. I'd go for slow walks beside low hedges, attempting to identify different blossoms by their scent. If I'd had a good week, or done something difficult, such as going to a party even though I was really nervous about it, or just told a friend that I couldn't go to the party without spending hours becoming convinced she'd hate me forever if I didn't go, I'd celebrate with a small bunch of flowers. I discovered that arranging them—or rather, preparing the stems so they would drink water, stripping them of extraneous leaves and trying to get them to sit nicely in the vase—made me feel calm and centered. I wasn't constantly thinking, or even trying to stop myself from constantly thinking. I was just enjoying a quiet moment with nature.

Last year, I was given a brilliant birthday gift—a place on a fancy arranging course. I took three days off, and looked forward to spending some time away from my emails, my

to-do lists and the slippery chaos of my brain. All I had to think about, for three days, was lovely flowers. Then I had a panic attack, half an hour before I was due to start.

What if I didn't have the right equipment? What if I'd got the time wrong, and I was late? I bet everyone else there had done courses before, or just had some instinctive, creative way with nature that eluded me. What if the teacher saw me and knew that I didn't belong? What if I had no one to eat lunch with? What if—and this was the big one—I turned out to be completely crap? What if my lovely, calming hobby was about to be ruined as I slowly realized I was actually a clumsy, fat-handed simpleton? This course wasn't cheap. What if it was a waste of money, and everyone was angry at me?

Still sobbing and sweating, I arrived early enough to buy a bumble-bee patterned apron. I don't think that panic attack could have been more quaint if I sang my list of fears in rhyming couplets, and accompanied myself with a ukulele.

It took me a while to calm down. The teachers and students were fine, but my anxieties kept springing up like worms emerging out of the ground after a rain storm. Was I standing in the right place? What if I forgot an important instruction? Would we run out of flowers? And then I got into the rhythm of what we were doing, turning my hand, layering stems, looping ribbon, starting over—it was mindful mindlessness. I felt soothed, and slowly became aware of the fact that I wasn't rushing to the end of the task. I was noticing the shape and scent of each bloom. A teacher said, "Ten more minutes!" and I didn't feel the familiar wave of nauseous panic that tends to accompany my deadlines. Eventually, I made something beautiful.

Objectively, I hadn't created a bouquet that could be sold in a florist's. It wasn't symmetrical, and my bow was slightly wonky. But, I'd chosen these roses, soft and warm as sun-bleached cotton, and the scented stock sitting in the center, looking a bit like a Post Office Tower for insects, smelling sensational. My hands had made something that my brain could appreciate without criticism, and it made me feel so calm.

You could pick any activity—quilting, cricket, metalwork, interpretive dance, making Fabergé eggs out of plasticine—and as long as it allows you to feel the joy of doing, and tune out the static of your brain, it's a valuable thing to practice.

However, I think it's really important to make sure you're focused on the way the activity itself feels and not the end result.

Beth, a teacher explains:

I used to love baking, because it's so soothing and measured. It forces you to be patient, pay attention and focus on exactly what you're doing at that moment in time. Then one friend asked me to make a birthday cake for her mum, and I ended up agreeing to do loads of stuff for other people. I really liked helping out, but I felt under so much pressure to make everything perfect that I wasn't feeling the benefit any more. The soothing part was lost. One night, I was stuffing envelopes for a school charity mail-out thing, and I realized it gave me the same relaxed sensation that I'd been missing!

Obviously, I didn't give up baking for envelope stuffing, but it did make me think about my priorities. I still make the odd birthday cake for very good friends, but I try to keep most of my baking for fun, and I feel so much happier. People tell me I could sell my cakes—it's really sweet of them, but I've realized that instead of making money, I'd rather protect the one part of my life that's for me, where I don't feel as though I'm under scrutiny!

Relaxing is hard, because in order to let go and feel good, we need to behave as if no one is watching, and we live in a world that has turned us all into exhibitionists—we're constantly on display. So, the first step to switching off is to find a hobby or an activity that is entirely for you, so that your enjoyment of the process is much greater than your anticipation of the result, and how that might be validated by other people. It's really hard but when we start to see that doing something—and sometimes doing nothing—is the vital part, not how it is documented at the end, we start to ease up and let go. We have a much better perspective on our place in the world once we stop obsessing about how we're seen. To relax, we must learn to dance, or cook, or nap, or arrange flowers, like no one's watching.

The big chill Shortcuts to relaxing times

Relaxation takes time, and if we had more time, we probably wouldn't need to relax so urgently. These relaxing shortcuts are very quick, effective ways to turn off your brain's deafening, anxious soundtrack and get some energy back into the rest of your body. I promise that you need not listen to a single wind chime.

If you have five minutes. Choose a song that you know all the words to, stick it on YouTube and dance like one of those inflatable-man balloons you see outside car showrooms. If you're at work, get your headphones on and dance in the toilet cubicle. You get bonus points for standing on the toilet.

If you have ten minutes. Masturbate, providing you have the space and inclination. It's much more relaxing than drinking a big glass of wine when you get home from work. (Go back and check out "A few words about wanking" if you need inspiration!)

If you have twenty minutes. Challenge yourself to learn a short poem—even if it's just a limerick. Recite it out loud. Make up a tune and sing it.

If you have an hour. Buy a pack of plain, un-iced cupcakes, and a box of icing pens. Go to town. If you want to create something dainty and delicate, follow your heart. However, if you've got a lot of stress to get out of your system, you might want to go fully Jackson Pollock on the cakes.

If you have a day. Cook yourself a three-course dinner for one. It doesn't matter whether you end up making beef wellington or jelly and ice cream, as long as you're having fun with the food. A day of puttering about and doing your own thing in the kitchen is a day well spent—even if things don't go to plan and you end up ordering takeout.

CHAPTER ELEVEN

How To Deal With Parents
(And Other "Real" Adults)

At my parents' silver wedding anniversary, my dad made a speech about my mum. "I cannot think of anyone who doesn't like her," he said sincerely. The tribute made me a little tearful. Mum, as she will now be known, despite the best efforts of my cheeky sisters, who sometimes refer to her by her first name in order to exasperate her, is highly likeable. Of course, I would say that, as her eldest daughter, but if I'm honest, I was well into my twenties before I could fully appreciate her many charms.

Mum is instinctively polite and kind. I have never heard her show off about anything, ever. She's quick, she's hilarious, she's an unbeaten Scrabble champion, she's one of the most well-read people I have ever met, and you have to try her lasagna. She's also a practicing Catholic, an upper-and-lower-case Conservative and a person with a pathological mistrust of gyms, fitted carpets, and the late Princess of Wales.

Lady Di is where our perspectives diverge. Mum objected to the dresses, the divorce, the drama, and I think the idea that a woman should be feted and celebrated for (what she sees as) the abandonment of her family and the pursuit of personal happiness. Whereas all I've ever wanted was to have my picture in the paper for wearing a tiara, and then be able to cry photogenically while Martin Bashir (any celebrity interviewer will do) does some sympathetic head tilting. Growing up, all the things I thought I liked—sequins, fusses, trying to turn myself into a tiny Elton John—seemed like the diametric opposite of Mum's favorite things: an hour's uninterrupted reading, a very cold gin and tonic, wearing jeans to a party. "You'll understand when you're older," she used to say, about everything from the confiscation of Eminem albums to the banning of a skirt that showed the bottom of my buttocks when I coughed. And now I do. Damn her!

As I was growing up, it was much easier to see myself in my father. Dad is quick where Mum is considered, extravagant where she is prudent, and inconsistent in a wholly human way. (Nothing made him more furious than a glass of milk spilled on a carpet, but he was very chilled out when I lost my flute at school.) He was the one who turned every trip into a Magical Mystery Tour, who wrote Christmas quizzes and birthday poems and silly songs to sing on holiday. He also has a stubborn streak that matches my own, and like mosquitos, we know exactly where to bite to achieve the most irritation.

I believe I have the best parents in the world, even though I spent some of my teens and twenties thinking they were the worst. I've learned to look at them differently, especially while I watch my friends figuring out their relationships with their parents. Ultimately, I think that part of being a happy adult involves working out what it means to be someone's child, and appreciating that relationship while you have the chance—if you have the chance.

In 2014, the Office of National Statistics found that a record number of young adults were living at home with their parents—approximately 3.3 million twenty to twenty-four-year-olds. Basically, it's because we're broke. High levels of unemployment, and starting salaries that won't cover rent, mean that many of us don't have the option of living where we'd like to.

Moving back home—if we ever had the chance to move out in the first place—may feel like failure, but you have to be pretty privileged to have that option. You need one or more parents who like you, have room for you and don't mind supporting you at a point when you, and they, had hoped you'd be supporting yourself. It's difficult to be an adult child who suddenly has to deal with reinstated curfews, parental pressure, and a limited amount of space. But it's just as hard for parents who find themselves held hostage by hungry young people who are old enough to drive and vote, yet immature enough to leave wet towels all over the floor.

Other countries have a culture of multigenerational living, but in the UK and US, we're still trying to make sense of it. I tried it briefly after getting fired from that first awful job. Some of my little sisters were still at school, so it wasn't too hard to slot back into family life. I wasn't disturbing an empty nest.

However, I soon discovered that living at home at twenty-three wasn't really any different from living at home at seventeen. I got told off for leaving lights on and not helping with the washing-up. I wasn't allowed to share a room with my boyfriend when he came to stay. My music was too loud, my skirts were too short and my shoes were too easy to trip over in the hall, but I don't remember doing any laundry, or cooking. I think I may have paid a tiny, token amount of rent but it probably didn't cover the cereal I ate every month.

Part of the problem was that both sides assumed the move home would be temporary, and we didn't work out how to establish a new relationship. I complained about being treated like a child, but is there anything more childish than being rescued from your first grown-up rental and staring balefully out at the highway while your piled-up pillows obscure your dad's view in the side-view mirror, tearfully complaining that everything is so unfair? I hadn't even bought those pillows; they'd been purchased by my parents before I started university.

I was so self-absorbed and upset that, at the time, I didn't give much thought to the fact that my parents were sad for me, and worried about me. If you're having a hard time, your parents or guardians are also finding it hard to see you struggle. They want you to get a proper job/partner/haircut because they think it might make you happy, not because they are sick of fending off questions from Auntie Heather. At twenty-three, I didn't know how lucky I was to have a mum and dad who would drive all the way from Dorset (to the house that we'd moved to in 1995) to the outer reaches of North London to rescue me, the daughter who was tripping over her first adult hurdle.

At the time, living with benevolent, bossy, fifty-plus roommates seemed like an endless, tedious punishment, but I look back at that period of my life with a mix of nostalgia and horror at my own ingratitude. My mum and dad won't be here forever, and I was lucky to have a little extra time to hang out with them. It wasn't all about me being too lazy to buy my own toilet paper. There was the hilarious, hideous game of Scrabble when it fell to Dad to explain to me what the word "quim" meant, and Mum's surprising fascination with Kanye West's debut album, "College Dropout", after one of us left the CD case in the car door. And the very enjoyable Sunday afternoon we spent learning how to make caipirinhas.

However, I'm aware that nostalgia is a dangerous mist that often causes us to move in the wrong direction and buy Keep Calm and Carry On key rings. It's easy to feel positive about that period retrospectively—but what's it like to be in it? I ask my friend Martha, who moved in with her mum and stepdad six months ago after breaking up with her boyfriend:

Well, first of all I think my experience is different from yours because it's just me at home—I don't have any brothers or sisters. So my parents had their lives set up independently before I came home. They were living as a couple and didn't have anyone else in their space. They've downsized—it's not the house I grew up in—and I'm in the spare room. At first, they were very welcoming, saying, "Of course, darling, you must come home!" but I think it's slowly hitting them that they're sharing the space now. They can't have people to stay at the weekend, because there's nowhere for them to sleep—and they can't dump laundry on my bed! Well, sometimes they do and then apologize resentfully.

We were lucky that we've always got on well as a family. I think that's why they offered. I love spending time with them, but I know that the circumstances aren't ideal. My stepdad is a lovely man. He married Mum when I was twelve, so I've known him for a long time. But he has children of his own, and I think he worries about where he'd put them if, hypothetically, they were in the same boat as I am.

I know the situation can't last forever. I'm really lucky—at the moment I pay rent, which Mum sticks in a savings account to go towards a deposit on a new place, so I'm being financially supported. I'm not earning a huge amount, and once I'd paid for rent and bills in a house share, I'd have very little to live on for the rest of the month. But I know this situation isn't great for any of us. We make it work by being very open and specific. I chip in with certain chores, I cook dinner a couple of times a week, I let them know if I'm going to be home late—but it does sometimes feel like living in a strict 1950s boarding house, albeit one with a flatscreen telly.

There are positives and negatives, but it puts a strain on the family dynamic. In the interests of objectivity, I talk to Helen, who is in her fifties. Her twenty-eight-year-old daughter has just moved out after living at home for a year:

It was the best of times, it was the worst of times! I think the biggest thing is that, as a mum, you do want your kids to be making their own way in the world. You love them, and in a way you'd love to have them with you forever, but you also know that's no fun for them and they should be discovering adulthood and enjoying those first freedoms. It's hard to do that when you're living with your mum. It's not fair on your generation at all, none of you earn enough money to move out and make plans.

The role of parent to an adult comes with its own set of challenges. I don't think kids realize that there's nothing we won't do for them. My daughter will still be my little girl when I'm seventy-six and she's forty-eight. We feel responsible, and we get exasperated with them, and when she leaves the TV on when she's out of the room or whatever, I do want to scream, "I didn't bring you up that way!" But now, she can have a crappy day at work, get home, pour herself a glass of wine and think about it on her own. When she lived here, it was hard for me not to involve myself in every drama. It felt like when she was at school all over again—I'd have to stop myself from offering to complain to her line manager!

It was a difficult year, but I loved it. I think—well, I hope—most parents would say that it's a pleasure to spend time with your children, no matter how old they are. And you get to see so many different sides of them when you see them every day. We'd have really good chats after dinner about

what was on the news, or the books we were reading. I'll al-
ways be her mum first, but when she lived here, we really de-
veloped a friendship, too. I think that we'll spend more time
together now for fun because we discovered a new dimension
to our relationship when she was back at home.

One of the hardest aspects of being an adult around older adults who see you as a child is that it's very difficult to be assertive.

Let's be honest, even if people are younger than you are, when they start talking to you in a way that is condescending to the point of being slightly parental, you're going to struggle to react to them. In your twenties, you simply can't scream, "IT'S NOT FAIR!" and then try to ruin their walls by putting up posters with thumb tacks. It might sound super obvious, but you must treat people as you wish to be treated. It's easy to act like a child until you get your own way, whether you're eight or twenty-eight, but it doesn't actually work when you're twenty-eight.

It's unlikely that the older people in your life will want to control the way you live, but it happens as Lizzie found out:

I moved back home after I lost my job, and I still argue with my
dad about how late I'm allowed to stay out. It's not as if I'm
constantly falling out of clubs, but recently I got home at 2 a.m.
on a Saturday and found him waiting for me at the kitchen ta-
ble, complaining, "What time do you call this? I was worried!"
I responded, "Dad, I'm thirty!" I'd had a few drinks, so obvi-
ously I was in no position to have a rational conversation about
his control issues. But at my age, I shouldn't have to pull that
teenage trick of "I'm staying with a friend tonight!"

I have some sympathy for Lizzie's dad—I suspect he's being trans-
ported straight back to her teenage years, and all the terror and anxiety

of being awake in the middle of the night, wondering whether your adorable, loving daughter is taking drugs down a back alley with bad men, even though she is probably just eating cheesy chips on a night bus or fighting with the friend who vomited in her shoes. But Lizzie's woes sound spookily similar to mine when I moved back home.

Once we're eighteen, we assume that we'll be considered grown-up enough to choose our own bedtimes.

When we're little, and our parents won't let us have what we want, their word goes. There isn't usually any room for negotiation. However, when we're having a disagreement with them, adult to adult—even if it is proper, established adult vs. new and uncertain adult—we need to work out a way of being clear and assertive about our needs, and reaching a solution that makes both parties happy and doesn't lead to any door slamming. When I've been in similar situations, I've imagined myself taking a deep breath, marching up to the person I'm struggling with and saying, loudly and slowly, "Now look here, my good fellow! This simply won't do!" and having my adversary giggle and roll over like a Labrador who wants a tummy tickle. For some reason, imaginary Assertive Me is dressed like the admiral from the car-insurance adverts.

However, being assertive is a shock for both sides. If you have to assert yourself with people who seem senior to you, they will almost certainly react badly at first. This is because they're not used to it, and will feel as though their status is being challenged, and they'll freak out, no matter how nice your approach is (and please do approach nicely!).

We all know the trick of sitting down together—adjacent, not opposite, because surprisingly it can seem confrontational when you're in a position to scream in somebody's face. We know that we need to find a neutral location, because most people might lose their shit in their own home, but can just about keep it together in a shopping center. But, until recently, I didn't think about my expectations, and the anticipated outcome. When you confront someone about a difficult issue, it's probably been in your head for days or weeks. You've brewed it to a Pantone shade of Lethally Caffeinated Tea, but you're asking them to consider the issue from an angle that is completely new to them. Your request might initially seem as shocking as offering them a peanut from a box that actually contains coiled snakes on springs.

Being assertive requires patience, and a lot of faith in yourself.

Leave your radical, shocking idea with them—for example, you say when you're going to be home late, and promise that you'll come in quietly and won't ever expect anyone to pick you up from outside Oceana, holding one shoe—and give the other adult the time and space to come to terms with it. It's easy to feel like a child in this scenario, but I promise that you won't if you hold on to the knowledge that you're making a reasonable request to an ultimately reasonable person. You're not going into battle with a monster who still won't let you have a Bratz lunchbox.

One thing that will enhance your relationship with your parents as an adult is other intergenerational friendships.

Sometimes this will happen organically—unless you work at a brand-new start-up, or you're one of fifty interns, you'll usually meet and make friends with older colleagues. You might work with people who are from the same generation as your parents, and your similarities, not your differences, will probably surprise you. When I found a job that made me happy, I loved working with older people who cared about what they did as much as I did—and I was astonished to discover that they respected my work and wanted to hear what I had to say.

When I needed their input, they were full of wisdom and advice, but they didn't let their seniority define our interactions, and as I started to see them as equals, I stopped seeing myself as a child in a grown-up world.

If you work for a company that offers any kind of mentoring scheme, it's definitely worth investigating it, and getting matched up with someone older and more experienced. We learn from our bosses and managers, but it can also be invaluable to learn from an adult who isn't directly affected by the way you work, because they'll be able to give you impartial advice. Most of us rarely have the chance to find an official mentor, so it's down to you to discover them as you go along. Asking someone you admire if they'd like to go for a coffee might seem scarier than going back to school and asking if the physics teacher you used to fancy feels like going to Pizza Express with you and your 2-for-1 voucher—but there isn't a person on the planet who wouldn't be flattered to be asked.

The worst thing they can say is, "No."

When we start to grow up properly, we often become closer to the adults in our lives than we were when we were children, because we're not necessarily looking to them for all the answers. We're slowly starting to understand that they don't always have any, and they're just as bewildered as we are—and like us, they have some experience but sometimes they're making everything up as they go along. When I was little, I thought my parents were all-knowing, all-powerful superheroes, but living as an adult means that I see them with new eyes, and realize that they're just as human and ridiculous as I am.

Yet, to me, that makes them even more super. I do think it's really important to develop friendships with people from different generations, inside and outside your family. When I'm struggling to feel like a proper adult, I feel better when I talk to a real grown-up, even if that person is telling me that she never feels like one, either, and all that the years bring you is perspective.

DAISY DOES THIS!

➤ My biggest regret about my time back at home is that I was a living embodiment of every parent's favorite cliché, and treated the place like a hotel. Seriously, I used to ask my mum for wake-up calls and I got in everyone's way by loitering in the hall to maximize the Wi-Fi signal. Now, I try to make up for it by being a good guest when I go home, and I bring flowers and wine, and offer to peel potatoes (although if I'm honest, I'm always hoping that we're having pasta).

➤ When I was little, my parents were constantly driving me to drafty church halls and collecting me from various play rehearsals and drama activities. Now that they no longer have children who need constant ferrying about, they've got into drama themselves, so I try to support them like they supported me by going to see their plays when I can.

➤ I ask adults for advice, and I *take* it. This applies to parents, relatives, old colleagues and people I meet through work. Anyone who has more life experience than I have will probably have a powerful perspective on something that I'm struggling with. Also, people adore it when you ask for advice, so it's a brilliant way to build strong intergenerational relations, whether I'm asking, "Should I quit this job?", "Should I get bangs?", or "How many eggs go in a quiche?"

➤ It's not necessarily a tip for everyone, but I fell in love with (and eventually married) a proper adult man. My husband is fourteen years older than I am, and he's taught me that legitimate grown-ups are very similar to brand new ones. We all watch the same movies, wear the same sneakers and overuse the word "awesome".

CHAPTER TWELVE

How To Be Sad

It's just after 9 p.m. on a damp day in the autumn of 2001. The curtains are drawn, the fire is lit, and Humphrey the cat has been shut inside the utility room after leaving one dirty protest too many inside Dad's slippers. The younger members of the family have gone to bed, and those over the age of thirteen are staying up to watch the medical drama *ER*. My family loves *ER*.

Some of us are into it because we're concerned about the relationship between Dr. Carter and Dr. Lockhart, and (rightly) fear that Dr. Kovač is on a mission to make a messy love triangle. Others have a gruesome fondness for watching grumpy doctors losing their arm to helicopter rotor blades. Everyone is united in their addiction to watching me weep. For me, *ER* has an emotionally pornographic quality, and I cry along as passionately as other people sing to their favorite parts of the *Sound of Music*. Made-up mothers dying in childbirth leave me ruined. Show me fictional people rescuing friends from fires only to die of smoke inhalation and my face becomes stiff with snot and saltwater.

Naturally, my sisters think this is hilarious. They nickname me "The Whale", and whenever something slightly sad happens, they turn to look at me and make big blinky faces, widening their eyes and mouths while making a high-pitched "HAWWWW" noise. Tonight is no exception. We're watching a father coming to terms with his daughter's rape, and I'm working my way through a box of Kleenex.

"Why do you even watch this when it makes you so sad?" gasps Beth. She's laughing so hard at me that she's on the brink of tears. (I find this deeply satisfying.) I'm trying to find an answer for her when a child actor is wheeled onto the screen on a gurney, and I start sobbing all over again.

Crying really is an awful hobby. It's not something you can talk about at parties—when someone has spent half an hour telling you about their snowboarding holidays, and eventually asks what you do for fun, I find it's easier to make something up than say, "When I really want to let off steam, I watch sad films about orphans and wail until my eyes are so swollen that I can't blink without experiencing a medical emergency!" Yet, this is how I spend my leisure time. Understanding and processing real pain seems terrifying, but synthetic sadness gives me release. As a teenager, I relied on sad stories. Immersing myself in imaginary emotions is what eventually prepared me to deal with my real ones.

Everyone wants to know how to be happy, but I think learning about being sad is much more useful. Happiness usually takes us by surprise. When you feel a delicious surge of joy, you don't wonder where it's come from. Some part of you might think, "Aha! It feels good to eat this delicious pie or laugh at this funny film! Hurrah!" But often there's no direct route to it. It's essentially random. However, we're all suckers for the idea that happiness has a formula.

Sadness strikes frequently, but when it comes to managing it, most of us haven't a clue. I'm sure a surprising number of us have sprinted from a party, consumed by nameless terror, and worked our way through a panic attack while holding onto a lamppost. But when sadness strikes on a Sunday afternoon, society says, "Cheer up!" and we're not really told how. It's taken all of my twenties to know that the worst thing you can do is to distract yourself from it. It's like thrush—the harder you pretend not to notice it, the thicker and smellier it gets.

In one of my favorite books, Nina Stibbe's *Man at the Helm*, the mother of the central character gives sadness a corporeal form. She calls it "the pig", and explains "the pig arrives when one's feeling fed up. He turns up first thing in the morning, and pins you to the bed—to make you think, to make you cry and make you see. You must make him welcome and he'll soon be gone."

I spent much of my teens and twenties running from the pig when I should have cuddled him close, and let him sit on my belly. Physically, I have tensed myself against sadness, bringing about even more misery and a bad back. Most of us will do anything—anything—to avoid sadness. The world wants us to be happy. We want to be happy. In a few scenarios, such as bereavements and break-ups, our negative emotions will be understood and tolerated for a limited period of time.

Otherwise, the universe conspires and manifests itself as a creepy man on a street corner yelling, "Cheer up, love! Got a little smile for me, baby?"

However, as soon as you allow yourself to experience sadness, and start sliding into it, you're moving closer to the end of the feeling. We need to learn to treat it like a stranger on a train. If you see a new passenger approaching and think, "I hope he doesn't sit next to me," he will sense your reticence and join you for a chat—probably about how he feels so much better now he has stopped wearing deodorant. But if you smile up at the stranger and pat the seat next to you invitingly, he won't stick around for long. Once we embrace all of our emotions, even the ones that scare us, they won't have nearly so much power over us. But where do we start?

Firstly, I think we need to stop seeing sadness as the opposite of happiness, and accept that we can't understand and appreciate our positive emotions unless we accept that they coexist with the tough ones. We'd probably all be much happier if we were better at allowing ourselves to be sad. A whole industry is devoted to making us all a bit cheerier. Like the diet industry, I'm sure some of the people involved have the best of intentions and genuinely want to improve the wellbeing of the world but it's hard not to be cynical, and I have to wonder whether a few of them are abusing their positions.

After all, they're in a position to make us feel as though happiness is the ultimate goal, and any sadness indicates that there's something wrong with us. Why encourage people to accept their emotions when you can profit from encouraging them to have better ones? For a long time, I have been the industry's plaything—I will spend anything up to £7 for an app that promises permanent contentment, even though I know I'd generate more personal joy from a free Google image search for "dogs in sweaters". I tried a gratitude app, and some days it did make me feel mellow and content—and some days it would crash and I would hurl my phone to the floor, screaming, "Fuck you, tiny Buddha!"

In this century, I think we're more aware and better educated about mental health than ever before. There are still issues with how we talk about it, the resources available to treat it and the fact that, weirdly, most of us are still more accepting and understanding about health conditions we can see, such as broken legs and stigmata. So, while we're getting better at understanding that depression is a serious issue, and treating it as such, we still suck at admitting that sometimes we all get a little sad, partly because the feeling is presented as a personal failing. If we feel that something's wrong, something must be wrong with us! It's isolating—you're trapped in a tower, staring out at a vast grey sky, hearing distant laughter and suspecting that everyone else is smiling in the sunshine.

In a way, I think our obsession with happiness is part of the problem. If I felt a bit blue for a few days, I used to think, "Oh, God, something is very wrong with me," and I'd treat my feelings like a dermatologist would tell you to treat a spot—I'd bury them under a big pile of ice, and then leave them alone. I'd keep smiling, and hiding behind my make-up, until everything became stiff and painful and erupted at the worst possible moment.

Anna, an old friend of mine, says:

I'm not sure where I first heard the phrase "Fake it 'til you make it" but I remember thinking about it a lot at school, and now it comes up at work. I was quite badly bullied by my best friends at secondary school. We'd been a close group for years, and one day I turned up and they suddenly started ignoring me, excluding me and spreading rumors about me. I talked to my form tutor who said, "Get a grip!" and told me that crying and being sad wouldn't solve anything. The only way I could get past it was to act as though I didn't care. So, I tried my hardest—and from then on, whenever I felt a twinge of sadness or uncertainty about anything, I'd stick my mask on. I've done jobs I've hated, but instead of allowing myself to acknowledge my unhappiness I've forged ahead and thought that if I forced myself to smile, I'd genuinely feel happier over time. I had a fight with my friend about my attitude. She said, "You just don't care about anything, do you?" and I yelled, "I'm not allowed!" then immediately burst into tears. It was an amazing breakthrough. I've just started seeing a therapist who has talked to me about "sitting within" my emotions, especially sadness, anger, and fear. I was so scared of feeling sad that I turned myself into a robot.

Something I've learned to love about sadness is the way it slows me down. For me, sadness can be so physically draining that I'm forced to sit still with it. My brain is too tired to see every different outcome, and so I feel low and lie low.

My friend Rachel thinks that listening to her body has helped her to learn to read her mind:

When I'm super sad, I usually feel very tired, achy, and generally run down. As soon as I feel slightly wobbly, I shut down. I try to have at least one day a month doing nothing, seeing nobody, and staying in bed with Netflix and an enormous sack of chips. Being sad makes me feel tired, so I get lots of rest. If I crave a particular food, I make sure I eat it. I keep hydrated, and I wear my softest jumpers because it makes me feel like I'm being hugged. About a year ago, I had a horrible break-up and it felt like the emotional equivalent of coming down with really severe flu—so I decided that I needed to create the emotional version of First Defense.

My hope is that embracing sadness makes me more compassionate. If a friend is feeling blue, I want to cheer her up and solve her problems, but I realize that's an arrogant approach. When I'm sad, I want the people close to me to acknowledge that my feelings are serious and significant, and I can only make this happen if I acknowledge it, too. Rachel adds, "Oh, God! Saying, 'Don't worry,' is like saying, 'Calm down!' It's done with the best will in the world, but it's never going to work. Why shouldn't I worry? It makes me feel like I'm not just dealing with feeling bad. I should also feel stupid for failing to find a solution to my woes, a solution so obvious to everyone else that they're telling me not to feel my feelings!"

I've had similar experiences to Rachel, and I think it helps to own the sadness. Instead of saying, "I'm fine," and hoping people will psychically read between the lines, I try to work out why I'm feeling sad (which isn't always possible) and tell people about it. Wear your sadness like a heavy cashmere overcoat—the kind you'd put on in 1942 if you were rich and cold and your lover had gone away to fight in the war. It's scary, but it's important to be open about the way you're feeling—conceal it, and you'll never get better, any more than you can cure a gangrenous leg by chucking a tablecloth over it and looking bemused when people ask, "What's that smell?" As you get better at identifying sadness and really letting yourself experience it, you'll develop a sense of the root causes and work out ways of managing them. Some of them will be unavoidable, but sometimes you'll discover that your whole world changes if you go for a lunchtime walk, or avoid Diet Coke after 4 p.m.

This approach of embracing rather than avoiding sadness has made me much better at managing all of my emotions. When I get angry, I allow myself to feel out of control. When I'm fearful, I tell myself that it's OK, and at least some of my concerns are rational. When I'm happy, I wallow in it and appreciate it. I know that happiness isn't the base state that I should be striving for, but a gift, and understanding what makes me sad has helped me to learn what makes me happy, too. Often it isn't what I was expecting. I love going out and spending time with my friends, but sometimes socializing leaves me feeling drained and anxious to keep up. A rainy walk in the park on my own sounds like the very definition of a sad activity but being out in the fresh air lifts my mood—a fact I discovered when I went on a bad-tempered, sulky stomp, thinking that getting cold and wet couldn't make me feel any worse. Leafy trees make me happy—even if they're growing above kebab shops and have carrier bags caught in the branches. Once you start letting yourself find the glad in your sad, you will turn into a complete hippy.

Some of the saddest moments of my twenties have marked significant personal firsts. Horrible problems—being fired, getting dumped, getting sick, having serious, scary fears and fights and freak-outs—are part of the structure of our lives.

We're going on a Bad Feelings Hunt and we can't go over them, we can't go around them, so we have to go through them. Feelings of devastation and desolation and of being consumed with sadness are a sign that a particular pain is especially acute because it's new. It might happen again, and it will feel horrible but if you can ride it out once, you know that the world isn't going to end.

I have a very clear memory of walking up a hill in the rain, the day after I was dumped by my good-friend-turned-terrible-boyfriend. The incline, and my lack of athletic prowess, was knocking the air out of my lungs, and I was making everything much harder for myself by weeping. It wasn't delicate, crystalline crying either, but snotty, open-mouthed gasping and honking. If other people had been on that stretch of pavement, they may well have called an ambulance, assuming I was in the throes of a respiratory attack. I didn't care about being seen or heard, or scaring the birds out of the trees. Crying was the only thing that I was capable of doing with my face. My world was ending, and I wanted to take my doomsday vibe to the streets.

It wasn't the first time I'd been in love and it hadn't worked out. At twenty-six, I could look back on a list of romantic disappointments and accept that most of my past relationships had ended for a very good reason. But I'd been so hopeful about this one, and it had gone so badly wrong. I couldn't imagine ever feeling so strongly about anyone else. I'd lost part of myself to that relationship, and I didn't think I'd ever feel as though I was enough when I was alone. Yet, as I walked, a tiny, helpful voice was whispering, "This is shaping you. This is the sort of excruciating emotional hell that, so far, you have only experienced in novels. If your favorite writers have been through this, and forged enough distance from it to write about it, it's probably not going to kill you."

I'd put my faith in a relationship that hadn't worked out. I'd spent so much time creating quick fixes for something that couldn't be saved, contorting myself into a shape that might fit into the life of someone who would not and could not love me. My sadness was strangely celebratory, because it marked the end of a long period of constant unhappiness. It was a sign that I'd finally acknowledged I couldn't pretend to be a different person for love—because what you have isn't love if you're doing it for someone who will never accept your true self. I'd been on a prolonged, painful learning period, and my tears meant that next time around, I'd know much more, and so the stakes would be higher. If my sadness was reaching its peak, perhaps happy times were on the way.

It took me a little while to figure things out. That was not the last time that I burst into tears while walking up a hill, or dancing at a festival, or trying on a skirt, or eating a Pret chef's salad. But, every time I cried made me feel a little bit better, as if I was starting to work out where I began and ended, having come out of a relationship that made me feel so lost. I wasn't crying only because he didn't love me; I was crying for who I was when I went in, and the hope and confidence she had.

Something vital in my nature had been crushed, and it was imperative that I learned how to nurture, protect and strengthen it so no one could harm it ever again. When I wept, I was watching the old relationship scab over. The process was patchy, flaky, and generally disgusting, but it was a sign of great healing, and it meant that soon I would be smooth and sorted out. That desperate sadness taught me to be patient with my emotions, and to accept that extreme distress is a bit like a flight delay. You can pace, complain and check the board every three minutes, or you can sit down with your book and make peace with the fact that you'll arrive when everything is ready for you.

Feeling sorry for yourself effectively is a real art. Some people will tell you that the best cure for heartbreak, melancholy, and even trapped wind is to focus your mind on other things, stay busy and go out and dig a ditch instead of dealing with what's bothering you. I've tried to do that, and it turns out I'm terrible at it. I need to allocate myself some serious wallowing time if I'm ever going to move on. I can't always just stop what I'm doing and go home for Netflix and Domino's, but I can plan precision wallows, and sometimes I can survive a bad Tuesday knowing I've lined up some seriously self-indulgent sulking for Thursday.

Here's how to plan your own wallow. Firstly, it's not a pamper night. Don't hold back on the face masks and fluffy flamingo slippers if it will make you feel better, but this is ultimately about you dealing with yourself at your worst, in order to feel your best. You're going to need a room with a bed, no people and no internet (you're allowed TV), and maybe a phone to use for ordering food. Clean pajamas might make you feel slightly more dignified, but I do some of my best, most effective wallowing in a giant T-shirt that came in a goodie bag and says: "check your selfie before you wreck your selfie". I think it's because there's no way I can leave the house while I'm wearing it, so it's an effective way of cloistering myself for the duration of the wallow.

Embrace the drama like your mum did when absolutely everyone got her theatre tokens for her fiftieth birthday. Cry like Drake himself is cheering you on. Remember, there's no one in the world who can make you feel worse about yourself than you! Play Texas Hold 'Em with your tragedy and play to win. During dark wallows, I have compared myself negatively to a woman in the middle of a paternity suit on Jerry Springer ("Two men are fighting over her! I have no one!"), to someone who'd just bought a house with chronic dry rot and a problem garden on an HGTV show ("I will never be a homeowner! Not for me the joy and pain of Japanese bindweed!") and everyone on The View ("They all have better hair than me!"). If it's at all feasible, a daytime wallow allows you access to the best television. Remember, it's a real opportunity for your irrational streak and narcissistic side to battle each other! Which is better?

On the assumption that you're generally a healthy, moderate person who is on nodding terms with the concept of vegetables, you're going to need takeout grease. Hot food will make you feel cocooned and cosseted. Snacks are great up to a point, but you'll find the self-loathing becomes worse, not better, when you get chips in the bed and have salty orange tidemarks on your wrist. Also, order what you know. I once had a notion that a Thai delivery would be a slightly healthier and heartier form of wallow sustenance, and used a place I'd never tried before, only to spend an hour panicking about whether they'd get lost, whether I had cash for a tip and whether they'd see my red, wet, puffed-up, Chelsea-bun face and run away at the door. ("I'm so useless and pathetic that I can't even have food delivered properly!") Also, the food wasn't that great and I ate my Pad Thai dreaming of Singapore noodles.

The beauty of the wallow is that eventually you start boring yourself silly, and start fancying a shower. I can't always remember what drove me to my bed, and, at some point, I get distracted by *Antiques Roadshow* and start realizing that my life cannot actually be all that bad, because I'm not collecting Toby jugs and displaying them in my home. Usually, once I've washed and put on some clean clothes, the wallow has done its job. A few years ago, some companies in the US tried to introduce the concept of "duvet days", and I don't know why they didn't catch on here. Most of us ignore our need to wallow because we feel as though we should be doing everything, every day. We don't break—we crash. I think it would be life-changing if we all accepted that most of us need to spend one day every couple of months embracing our "I can't even" feelings, and just stopping for a bit.

The next question is what do you do if you try a wallowing day, and set aside time to let yourself feel your feelings, but the sadness doesn't lift?

The number of young people dealing with depression is increasing every year. It's a desperately misunderstood illness for which it's hard to get help since there isn't a lot of public funding for treatment. Also, when the act of just living is exhausting, it can be incredibly difficult to identify what you need to get better, and to find it.

A 2015 Cambridge University study found that colds and depression have a lot in common. They're both caused by inflammation within the body, making us feel listless, lethargic, and vulnerable. We'd all prefer to avoid colds entirely, but most of us succumb at some point, no matter how many vegetables we eat or how frequently we douse our hands with anti-bacterial sanitizer. We can try to alleviate the symptoms but we usually just have to accept that a virus takes its time and can't be chased out of the body before it's ready to leave.

I've experienced some depressive episodes, usually alongside my anxiety disorder. I'll burn up all my energy on worrying, and then find myself stuck in a miserable slump—I'll briefly get angry with myself for doing so little, try to go to the gym and sink down into despair again, defeated by trying to summon the energy required to lace up one sneaker. These moments have become much shorter and easier to manage ever since I started trying to listen to myself a bit more. My inner voice used to be a semi-retired sergeant major, the sort who had gone on to run fat camps for wealthy, zaftig children, and it would shout, "STOP THAT, YOU WORM! GET UP! YOU HEARD ME! WHAT HAVE YOU GOT TO BE SO DEPRESSED ABOUT? STOP WHINING, GET DOWN AND GIVE ME TWENTY!" (At this point another inner voice would interrupt and say, "Twenty what? You want four high fives?")

I haven't been able to get the sergeant major to leave the mental premises, but I have added a yoga teacher to the internal speaker rota, who stares him down and tells me, "Work with the body you have today! Push yourself—but stop when there's resistance. It's better to do a little bit, and do it right, than it is to rush to the end and risk hurting yourself." Happily, she has not yet tried to sell me crystals and coconut water.

Our mental health is a matter of utmost seriousness, and I believe that the lives we live now put us all at an increased risk of experiencing problems in the future, as well as the present. However, if we can work to understand and embrace our own emotions, I'm sure we'll be in a stronger position and able to ask for support when we need it, as well as supporting ourselves.

If we're ever going to understand ourselves, we need to understand that there will be times in our life when we feel deeply, profoundly sad. Sometimes there will be a "good" reason, and sometimes there will be "no" reason. All we can do is be still in the eye of the storm. To extend the metaphor, it's about learning how to be an emotional meteorologist getting perspective on the personal weather system, instead of attempting to open a flimsy umbrella and feeling small and hopeless when it gets blown inside out. Most importantly, even though sadness is an emotion of isolation, it's one of the most universal feelings. It can be deeply comforting to remember that if you're racked with misery, you're in good company.

DAISY DOES THIS!

> ➤ If I can concentrate, I read. When I'm feeling really sad, I turn to the beloved books that I almost know off by heart, and I find them deeply comforting. This is especially true when the characters deal with difficult emotions and come through them. Some of my favorites are *Rachel's Holiday* by Marian Keyes, *The Pursuit of Love* by Nancy Mitford and *Rivals* by Jilly Cooper.

> ➤ I go for a walk. Anything really dreadful doesn't seem quite so acutely sad when I'm surrounded by green leaves and fresh air, and I'm able to examine the emotion instead of drowning in it. Also, it's hard to feel like everything will be completely terrible forever if you're in a park surrounded by adorable dogs.

> ➤ I write it down. I don't let anyone read it, but sometimes coming up with the words I need to explain the sadness forces me to analyze what's going on and process it properly.

> ➤ Sometimes, I catastrophize. So, everything is terrible, and I am miserable. What if I were on fire? Or my family were all being held captive by a brand-new boy band who were torturing them by playing irritating earworm songs, on a kazoo? Or I'd recently had a sexy moment in a log cabin, and an unshiftable splinter was lodged in or around my, er, kazoo? If I think about what could be worse, it helps me to see the sadness for what it is, and to trust that it will eventually pass.

CHAPTER THIRTEEN

How To Be Jealous

I am frequently, horribly envious. At some point I think I've been jealous of everyone I know. In the past, there was the standard, "Ah, they're getting married and I've just been negged by a man on match. com whose profile picture is a selfie he took while doing community service." Or, "That person is buying a house, and I'm over my overdraft limit and the closest thing I have to a cash asset is the £4.87 I've collected in Boots Advantage Points."

Then there's the stab of pain I experience about four times a day when someone writes something incredibly brilliant and I hate myself for not thinking of it first, or I hate myself for knowing I would have been incapable of thinking of it in the first place. I envy my little sisters for their quick wit, encyclopedic movie knowledge, and ability to wear a range of nude shades and look like a Kardashian and not a person who has been dared to make up using nothing but the contents of a first-aid kit. I'm jealous of my friend Lauren for her silky blonde mermaid hair and ability to sew patches onto her jeans that make them look like Gucci originals. (If I had a go, I'd look like a very confused Brownie who didn't understand that her badges were supposed to go on a sash, and not her legs.)

I'm envious when I go on the Ikea website and think about everyone in the world who keeps their possessions neatly and attractively on shelves and racks, and doesn't spend every morning falling out of bed and stumbling through a pile of books and dirty knickers. I'm envious of minds and bodies. Before she died, I envied Mother Teresa for doing so much good for so many people ("She makes me feel like a total evil failure!") and obviously, I'm jealous of everyone I follow on Instagram.

We know jealousy is not a positive force. It's toxic, draining, and it makes life difficult. Theodore Roosevelt is believed to have said, "Comparison is the thief of joy," and comparison is where jealousy plants its dark, stubby root. The more time and energy we devote to wanting what other people have, the less there is to devote to our own happiness and peace.

However, knowing jealousy is bad for me doesn't stop me from feeling it, any more than knowing too much wine is bad for me stops me from pouring a fourth glass if I'm in a particular mood. Ever since I was little, I've been told that jealousy is a wrong feeling, and I shouldn't entertain it. We should strive to be envied, not envious. As a result, I spent my twenties playing Whack-A-Mole with my emotions, feeling bad because everyone seemed to be doing better than I was, and feeling worse because I knew I was being negative and nasty. My jealousy was simply a sign of my weakness, and I had to hide it.

What would happen if we all admitted we felt jealous of each other from time to time? If we accepted that it's the inevitable consequence of being endlessly pressured into comparison, especially because we constantly pit women against other women? Let's imagine that we heard Meryl Streep saying, "When I was younger, I was totally jealous of Goldie Hawn—I was expected to be serious all the time, and she got all the fun, sexy roles." Admittedly, it's unlikely, but the hypothetical thought makes me feel as though my suppressed emotions were vacuum packed like coffee beans, and someone has just snipped at the seal. I experience the most corrosive jealousy when I'm struggling with the pressure to be perfect. If I had more evidence that "perfect" people felt it, too, I'd be doing the emotional equivalent of unbuttoning my skinny jeans and breathing out.

I think the biggest problem with jealousy is that it makes us so distracted. Sometimes I'm envious of people because they're doing something I've been dreaming about. More often, the jealousy has a novel quality. "I'd never even thought about wearing a big hat," I'll mutter, "but I would cheerfully kill that Instagram stranger for her massive straw boater." In a way, I think that these feelings are mainly just signals that we're alive, awake and have a healthy interest in the world around us. But they can be damaging, causing us to swerve off course and to lose sight of our destination entirely.

I've experienced jealousy that overwhelmed me entirely, a tidal wave of frightening feeling that knocked me to the ground and dragged me under water. There have been moments when I simply couldn't switch it off, despite my best efforts, and I was completely consumed by the idea that everyone else seemed to be living their best life, and I was living my worst. But it fades. Life can take you by surprise in the loveliest ways. You can get to the end of a period of intense envy and suddenly discover that you're just too happy and busy to be jealous any more.

Amy, a psychology lecturer, explains:

Engagements were the worst for me, for a long time. I spent three years in a really difficult relationship with a guy who made this huge deal about not wanting to commit, and how no woman was going to tie him down. He'd often say things like, "I think I love you, but I'm not sure if I'm in love with you"—he was massively manipulative, and I felt desperate and worthless. All I wanted was a sign that he cared, and every Facebook engagement felt like an announcement saying, "This person is loveable, and you are not."

Finally, I saw sense and dumped the bad boyfriend, and I was so much happier—but I didn't realize how much until an old schoolfriend got engaged, and I was filled with positive feelings and good wishes for her. It took me ages, but I found some perspective and realized that another person's good news is not a judgement on my lifestyle.

Jealousy had been such a big part of my life, and I felt like I'd really grown up and moved on when I stopped feeling it so acutely. Admittedly, it hasn't gone for good. I still get the odd pang when I think about how much I'd like to meet someone amazing, but every engagement reminds me that I'm doing what makes me happy by not wasting my time with someone who puts me down.

Like Amy, my struggles with jealousy have signified that some part of my life is out of order. Also, I've come to learn that the more jealous I feel, the more likely it is that I don't know the whole story—someone's success has usually come about after a series of struggles. Whenever I've asked people about their spectacular achievements, they have a litany of perceived failures lurking below the surface, things they have worked hard on that haven't gone as well or helped them to meet their goals. I don't know anyone who is doing well who hasn't had moments when they've doubted themselves. You show me someone you're jealous of, and I'll show you someone that person is jealous of.

Katya, an actress, tells me:

I have one friend who went to drama school with me, hated it, decided that no part of performing was for her and that she wanted to go into something much more stable. She's an administrator in a hospital, and her life is very together. She's one of the people that I love most in the world, but sometimes when we hang out, I feel almost faint with envy when she tells me about her routine, her colleagues, and her ability to save money—especially if I've had a quiet period, and spent weeks mooching around, maybe doing some waitressing. She often says, "I'm so glad I quit. I couldn't do what you do. This really suits me!" and it makes me wonder whether I made a bad choice. Is she secretly laughing at me? Did I make a big mistake in pursuing this as a career? I love what I do, I couldn't not do it, and I know that if I worked in a hospital, it would probably finish off the NHS in about four days. But knowing the envy is irrational doesn't stop me from feeling it. It makes me question myself.

It's interesting that Katya's jealousy becomes especially acute when she's feeling insecure about her career. When we're not getting what we want, and what we're working for, we tend to internalize the feelings and wonder if we're the problem. Did we pick the wrong path? I'm sure that when Katya is doing work she loves, she doesn't give hospital administration half a second's consideration. Envy rarely visits when life is good, but when we're worried about the future and desperately struggling to maintain our integrity and identity, it can do some serious damage.

Also, I wonder whether Katya's mate feels the need to defend her choices. Maybe she can't help speculating about what her life would be like if she'd stuck with something challenging, and worked through it, instead of giving up. Perhaps she feels the need to stick up for her sensible job because she's slightly envious of Katya's glamorous, more precarious one. In many situations, quitting can be the smartest, most sensible thing a person can do, but thinking about what might have been and wondering "what if" is a real envy trigger. Usually, if a choice is hard, it's because there is no obvious answer and no clear path to take. If you spend too much time wondering about the people moving in different directions, it can become impossible to move forward.

Katya says that instead of fighting the jealous feelings, she's done her best to accept them, and understand them:

Am I envious of the fact that she spends all day looking at budgets on spreadsheets, and has a brilliant working knowledge of Excel? No. Am I jealous because she knows she's getting paid at the end of every month, keeps regular hours, and always has someone to eat lunch with? Yeah, a bit. But I've decided to do the job that makes me happiest in the world, and right now I'm choosing that over being bored but solvent. I've fixed the lunch thing by arranging a weekly date with another lonely freelancer. And actually, I feel a bit more confident and sure of myself by thinking about it and realizing that I choose to live and work the way I do, and that's no bad thing.

If you are feeling a little lost, thinking about the people you're jealous of and why can be strangely life affirming. When I wrote about clothes and fashion, I admitted to having a difficult relationship with Instagram, and that I sometimes spend hours stalking gorgeous girls who take perfect selfies and have thousands of followers. To observe and appreciate beauty is something that should bring me great joy, but it can trigger so many toxic thoughts that it makes me feel totally poisonous. Where is my multimillion-pound house to pose in front of? How come their bone structure is so delicate that they look as though their faces were spun by a spider, when mine is like a toddler modeled it with raw cookie dough? Their sky is better than my sky.

Then sometimes I think, "You know what? I am really into my own hair today, and I love this dress. It's the first time I've worn it, and I'm happy! I'm doing a selfie!" I take a picture, and I see a cheerful, attractive girl—someone who looks as though she knows how to have a nice time, a person who is fun and friendly and loved. I post it, and people like it. I can look at myself and think, "There are days when I would feel really negative about this person." Future Me will have some sort of crisis of confidence, whether that's a professional rejection, a family fight or a big spot on my chin, and think, "Urghh, I hate that Past Me, smiling in the sunshine, being all smug. She thinks she's so great." Then I wonder about Distant Future Me, and decide that she's probably capable of doing something so brilliant that Past and Present Me would be so overcome with jealousy that we'd have to arrange to meet in a pub, specifically to criticize her.

Jealousy, at its very heart, is the failure to feel self- compassion. When we're struggling to feel good about ourselves, watching other people get the things we want is going to make us feel worse. We see only obstacles, and reasons why we can't live the life we'd like, which is partly why we sometimes think that a successful person has stolen our triumphs from us. It's illogical. We're not Top 40 singles, being stopped from going up the charts because one particular person is always number one. Success is like a spaghetti supper cooked by a stereotypical Sicilian grandmother—there is more than enough for everyone, even though some of the people at the table already seem full of it! If you're generally happy and secure, a dash of envy can spur you on. If you're already struggling with self-esteem, it can ruin your life.

My worst, most debilitatingly jealous moments have always been fueled by the sense that I am simply not enough on my own. If you define your worth as a human by your achievements—as I have often done—of course you're going to feel like total shit when someone does something bigger and better than you have.

For years, I was obsessively jealous of another writer who worked for a rival magazine. I barely knew her, but I knew she was my opposite number—we were both junior writers, and the nature of the work we did was very similar. I was curious about her. One day I discovered that she had been promoted to Entertainment Editor, and I cried. From then on, I decided that she was better than I was, and she knew it. (Of course she didn't. She had no idea who I was.)

Then came the news that she had started a job on a huge, national title—a job I'd seen advertised and thought, "I'd really like to do that, and maybe I'll be ready to apply in about five years' time." Then she left that because she'd been headhunted to launch a new magazine.

My being jealous of her was the closest thing I had to a proper hobby. We had a few mutual friends and acquaintances, and everyone adored her. "No one is that nice! I bet she's secretly evil, and kicks puppies and puts curses on people in her spare time," I'd think. "She must be rude to waiters, or one of those people who never gets a round in, or something." I knew that she was petite and slender, and told myself that she must be using her gorgeous good looks to get ahead. "It's not fair! I'd be having my dream career, too, if I didn't have this massive butt!" I'd complain.

Eventually, I came to terms with the fact that I was still a junior writer, and if I wanted to do anything about that, I'd just have to leave my job and see what happened. My own career became absorbing, challenging and exciting to me, and stuff started to happen. I'd found the right lane, and I finally felt as though I was driving with the top down and the music pumping, on a mission to break the speed limit. Then I ran into my old "enemy" at a party.

Obviously, she had no idea that I used to spend so much time thinking about her—at least, if she did, she was even more generous and lovely than previously advertised. If she knew the truth, she would have been well within her rights to have me removed from the building. She was just a girl, like me. A beautiful, funny, clever, charming girl who was incredibly good at her job, and had every right to celebrate her successful career. I'd imagined meeting her so many times, and predicted the conversation. "As one of the most sought-after journalists in this country, I shouldn't even be talking to pond scum like you!" she would say. "I'd give you career advice, but you're too terrible to take it. I wouldn't be surprised if you were an intern forever, or until your magazine folds thanks to your incompetence!" she'd hiss, before turning from me, with a swish of an enormous mink cloak, as a team of footmen dashed over to make sure that I hadn't accidentally breathed on her and contaminated her with inferior writer germs.

In real life, she told me that she'd loved writing for teens, too, and that she was about to start freelancing because she preferred writing to editing, and she was really nervous about how she was going to pay her rent, and how she'd cope in quiet times. I felt hugely humbled, and horrible about my litany of backed-up bitchy thoughts. She was a glorious, graceful example of someone who knew exactly who she was, and stayed true to it. She believed in writing, hard work, honesty and kindness. She was brave enough to take a risk, because she understood the difference between the sort of success that means everyone thinks you're great, and the kind that is just about doing the thing that makes you really happy. She was an advert for staying in the right lane, not zooming off, trying and failing to catch up with the wrong things because from a distance they look shiny and exciting, and someone else is driving them.

In a way, I'm sad that I'd spent so long thinking mean, and frankly crazy, thoughts about this brilliant woman, and envying someone who might have made an amazing friend. On the other hand, I'm glad that I experienced jealousy at its most extreme; otherwise, I wouldn't understand that it has so much to teach us. Envy has brought me peace and perspective, and led me to a positive place. It's only because I've experienced the damage it can do that I know how it can hold me back, and how important it is to remember quietly, "I am good," instead of screaming, "Everyone else is better."

Twelve jealous thoughts you will have while scrolling your Instagram feed

There's regular envy, and there's Insta envy—the ravenous, insatiable beast that feeds on your desire for shiny hair and happy holidays, leaving you feeling like an unworthy worm who is incapable of creating a single simple quinoa bowl. If you've ever experienced serious selfie envy or hashtag rage, at least one of these thoughts will have crossed your mind mid-scroll.

I bet that coffee had gone cold by the time she'd finished editing the picture of it.

Obviously, nothing says love like mashing your face against someone's chin. I hope her boyfriend has nits, and they colonize her hair extensions.

She's used so many filters here that it looks like she's making a racist statement.

Why is it captioned "My trip to Paris!" when it's just a big picture of her face!?

Yeah, that quote is inspiring. It's inspired me to smash my phone screen.

#Is #She #Capable #Of #Functioning #Without #The #Hashtag #Key #?

Does that cat have poo on its bum? Did she document it before she cleaned it? Should I call the ASPCA?

Yeah, her kids are #supercute. Shame their dad is always putting racist memes on his Facebook wall.

That's not #champagne, that's cava.

Oh, she was at a wedding? Was there a human bride and groom, or was it the marriage of her shoes?

Nice lobster dinner? Are Arby's doing lobster now?

She cannot put it up again and tag it "throwback Thursday" just because it didn't get enough likes on Tuesday.

DAISY DOES THIS!

➤ When I notice I'm feeling a twinge of jealousy, I don't try to shut it down straight away. I explore it. Instead of feeling guilty about the bad feeling, I wonder what my brain is trying to tell me and try to break down the jealousy into its component parts.

➤ If I'm jealous of people I don't know very well, I try to make friends with them! As soon as I start to get to know them, I can understand their journey and appreciate their work, and learn what has led them to all the moments that are making me envious. If I'm jealous of someone, I'm usually a bit frightened of that person—once I get to know them, I realize there's nothing to be scared of.

➤ I see jealousy as a sign that I need a bit more love in my life. I try to slow down and stop chasing after achievements that will help me to prove I'm just as good as everyone else. Instead, I fill my time with big baths and long walks, and try to focus on the fact that I don't need to do anything. I'm enough if I exist just as I am.

➤ Sometimes I'm jealous of a friend, so I open up and tell her about it. This stops good relationships from turning toxic, and can often lead to a really helpful, reassuring conversation. Jealousy can feel incredibly isolating—it makes me feel like I'm trapped on a hostile island, and when I know that other friends experience it as badly as I do, it's like they're coming to rescue me with a really robust dinghy.

➤ If nothing else works, I find a picture of the subject of my jealousy and give that person a full, lavish Biro beard. It's not very grown-up, but it's really satisfying.

CHAPTER FOURTEEN

How To Make And Manage Money

There is one upside to irrational terror, and it's this: you can be scared of the most specific, obscure thing in the world and it usually has an impressive Greek name. I'm hugely grateful that I'm not trychophobic (afraid of hair) or trypophobic (holes), but if someone was telling me they couldn't use colanders because the holes trigger their trypophobia, I'd be equally sympathetic and impressed. It sounds so fancy!

However, I've looked all over the internet and I can't find a grand, academic word for the weird and debilitating fear that dominated my twenties—fear of ATMs. I've struggled my way through some astonishingly toxic relationships. I've had problems with men, sex, alcohol, my own body and mind, but the worst one of all, by a long way, is my connection with money.

We all struggle to keep track of our spending. We live in a world where money is power and wealth propels us, and we have to learn to make good, responsible choices while using it to get the stuff we want—food, shelter, and Beyoncé tickets.

All the financial advice I've ever been given has been practical. I've been in tears, not knowing how I can afford to get to work without hiding in a train toilet and using a series of fake accents to confuse the guard, and a well-meaning person would say, "Your problem is organization! You need a budget, and a spreadsheet of your incomings and outgoings!"

My problem was that I didn't earn very much because I didn't think I was worth very much. I didn't know how to ask for more money in a way that proved I deserved it. My problem was that I was already economizing by eating rice for dinner every night, because an old roommate had left a big jar of it behind when she moved out. My problem was that I was constantly applying for jobs that might pay me more money, but I'd always hear a "no" if I heard anything at all. Every rejection made me less confident about the next application. I was so scared and miserable that every so often I'd snap and buy a new dress or a round of drinks on my credit card because I was so fed up with trying and failing and feeling so horribly aware of my brokeness all the time.

The first time my debit card was declined, the machine flashed a message urging me to contact my bank. I did not want to contact my bank. I already knew what they were going to say. "You're a liability, we're shutting your account down, your only option is to go home and live with your parents." I could not even think about throwing myself on the mercies of my family, because there was so much they didn't know, and I felt too ashamed to tell them.

There was the loan I'd taken out to move to London. I'd burned through all my money when I was studying, even though I'd had huge amounts of parental support. The credit card I'd taken out "for emergencies" was stretched to the breaking point. I had yet to get to the end of a month without meeting an emergency. My family looked after me for long after they were obliged to, and I knew that they had saved up and made sacrifices so that I could live the life they'd dreamed of for me. They were so proud of their eldest daughter and her promising career, and the fact that she wrote for a living—something they would both have loved to have done. But I wasn't really making a living. I was lying to them, and lying to myself. I wanted to believe that staying late at work and saying yes to everything would bring me a pay rise and a promotion, and that the chance to prove myself was right around the corner. All I was proving was that I didn't believe in myself enough to shout my worth and stop simply doing as I was told.

I made more and more purchases on my credit card through fear of using my bank account. I'd walk miles out of my way to find a shop where I could get cash back because the idea of getting money from a hole in the wall made me feel so scared I thought I was going to pass out. Bank statements and credit-card bills piled up, and I stacked them in shoe boxes, carrier bags, and even opaque Tupperware containers because I couldn't bear to see them, and any familiar financial logo printed on an envelope made me want to vomit. I shoved them into a "drawer of doom" at the bottom of my wardrobe, pushing them through a tiny slit at the top when the drawer would no longer fully open. I stared at the poor postman with a look of open hostility. Deliver me from deliveries!

I don't think I opened a letter from the bank or the credit- card companies for a whole three years. I moved around with my envelopes in a secret suitcase, weighed down by twenty kilos of fear and self-loathing everywhere I went. I was the one who prided herself on being honest to the point of excessiveness, so I felt like a total hypocrite. I'd tell you how to have multiple orgasms, how I'd once got so drunk that I'd sleepwalked to a chest of drawers in the night and peed all over my boyfriend's socks, how I'd been thrown out of the Groucho club for standing on a sofa and reciting a Dorothy Parker poem, and how I'd once been stood up for a date by a friend's baby brother, but no one could know that I was broke. No one must suspect that I didn't go for long walks in the rain for romantic reasons, but rather because I didn't want to spend a pound on a bus ride; or that I'd buy dinner for everyone with my credit card because I was too scared to admit that I couldn't pay cash for my own. I'd happily admit to masturbating if I couldn't sleep, but not that my sleeplessness was caused by my fear of being so far in the red that my bank might have me sent to prison.

When we shrink away from the things we're afraid of, we shrink ourselves. Worry about money usually comes from a logical, rational place, but my imagination was allowing my worry to grow to grotesque proportions, beaming it to every corner of my universe until it filled a whole sky. I hid from it, and when I ran out of hiding places, I took pains to become small and slow. I did everything the long way and the hard way, spending four hours trying to scan some old bank statements to send to a new landlady because I couldn't bring myself to look at the screen while I worked, or getting off at the wrong tube station and adding an hour's walk to my commute because I'd heard a rumor that someone in the center of town was giving out free shampoo.

Once, I was sent into paroxysms of panic on a date when I'd used the last of my cash to pay for dinner, and didn't have an extra £6 for an impromptu gig on the way home. If I hadn't been so freaked out and worked up about money, I could have just said I didn't have any, but it was easier to pretend I suddenly had a stomach upset than to explain that my bank card didn't work. Then the date tried to put me in a taxi, and I made up another lie about needing fresh air, rather than revealing that I'd be financially ruined if I tried to cover my cab fare.

Then, as you know, I sort of lost my job.

Although I really wasn't sure about my boss's suggestion to go freelance, I knew the office was full of junior staffers and interns who earned even less than I did and I wasn't going to get the pay raise I desperately needed. If I left, they could give me enough work to cover my rent, almost, and at least I'd save some money on the expensive commute, or so I reasoned. "Just make sure you get lots of contacts, and save up some money, and you'll be fine!" I was told. What great advice! So achievable and realistic!

I threw myself into writing, seeking out work, agreeing to do absolutely everything that came my way and emailing everyone I had ever met, claiming that I had the insight of Dickens, the imagination of Coleridge, and the ability to type faster than I could talk (the last one was true). Away from the office, and train rides, team drinks and mandatory birthday-present envelopes, my outgoings shrank. I was so frightened for my career that I worked ferociously, and I discovered freelance jobs that paid better than staff ones.

Still, I didn't look at my bank balance. Still, I'd have to shut my eyes tight if I walked past a cash machine, convinced that a spectral Money Monster would reach out and grab me with a chilly fist, and sit me down in front of a bank manager who would decree that I was a bad human being and all of my resources were being shut down.

Now I know that bank managers are like gynecologists—they really have seen everything. If you're at all worried, make an appointment to talk things through. You're their customer. They want to help and they won't shout at you. But when I was a teenager, I was obsessed with Kafka's novel *The Trial*, and I could quickly convince myself that I was always on the brink of being arrested and persecuted by a faceless government and stripped of my identity, possessions, and name. I'd imagine buying a brand-name moisturizer from the drug store, typing in my PIN and then being blinded and deafened by flashing lights and alarms as a cage descended, before I was hauled in by the authorities. "Frivolous BITCH! How dare you buy non-essential items! This ends now! Where you're going, there won't even be soap!" someone would shout at me—weirdly, in my head, this person looked exactly like Darth Vader.

When I met the man who became my husband, I could tell that he thought it was a little bit odd that I never used ATMs, and that if someone mentioned money, I'd change the subject as quickly as I could, regardless of how clunky and disjointed the segue was. (Once, a discussion at a dinner party about savings accounts led to me frantically interjecting, "Or, um, windows! Gosh, you really know how to get your windows clean! Um, what do you use?" Everyone gazed confusedly at me, and then at the nearest window, which was caked in pigeon crap.)

Then, he asked me to help him with a difficult favor. He hadn't been paid for some work for an overseas contractor because of a banking glitch. He'd been advised to get it sent to a different account, and he wanted to try mine.

How can you tell the person you love that you've lied to them? How do you explain that you think you might be in the biggest financial mess since Steve Carell started shouting at estate agents in *The Big Short*, that you have no idea how much money you have or owe and that sometimes you sneak to the bathroom at night so you can cry about it all without waking him up?

I couldn't. Instead, I agreed and spent the next few hours quietly weeping and vomiting. It was easier. The next day I walked to the actual, physical bank, because when you find money more frightening than a wet Gremlin, having access to online banking is about as appealing as filling your bathroom sink with someone else's diarrhea before you brush your teeth. I'd assumed that the transfer was going to be swallowed up by my unauthorized overdraft, the bank manager would close in on me and I'd have to write and apologize from a police cell.

My heart thumping as sweat poured off my forehead, I stuck the card in the slot and selected the option I'd been avoiding for a thousand days. Check balance. The world was ending, the sky was falling in, I was in credit!

At this point, I'd been doing some corporate copywriting and pulling in a regular income, but I'd never let logic soothe my anxieties, and I wasn't going to start now. I'd been earning more and spending less, but I was truly astonished to discover that I was out of my overdraft and out of the woods. I had safety money. If I ran out of work, I could still pay my rent. If I wanted, I could book a flight to New York without using my credit card. I had a message from the bank, who wanted to know whether I would like to set up a savings account. I could be the sort of person who had savings!

I ran out of the bank feeling like Scrooge on Christmas morning. The ghosts were gone, and the biggest turkey in the window was mine for the taking! Still not entirely convinced that the nightmare was over, I ran to a cash machine and requested not ten, not twenty, but £50 sterling. It came out!

My story of financial doom and disaster had a happy ending, but it is not an instructional tale. If I hadn't been forced to check my balance on that day, not long after my twenty-eighth birthday, I'd still be starting stupid conversations about windows and buying M&S multipack batteries in order to make up the minimum spend to get cash back on my card. I felt frightened and powerless, so I demonized my fears and allowed them to become much bigger than I was. Bank managers aren't baddies, and if I'd asked for help, I might have been advised to consolidate my debts or apply for a bigger authorized overdraft, but I wouldn't have been taken down in a cloud of poison gas and shuriken ninja throwing stars. My relationship with money reminded me of grappling with an eating disorder, starving myself for days until I couldn't take any more and had to go on a big binge, and constantly trying to be "good", getting angry with myself for being "bad" and hating myself for not keeping up. Instead of setting myself realistic goals, I'd just say to myself, "You are a big fiscal fuck-up. It's no wonder you're so bad with money, you're a bad person," then wonder why it felt as though everything was going wrong.

I'm still engorged with guilt about the fact that I got myself into an awful situation and I grew up with sensible, kind, generous parents who did their best to teach me about saving, and were always there to support me when times got tough. It isn't fun being embarrassed and ashamed about asking your parents for cash, but at least I knew they were able to help out. I started out with more than most people, and I still made a mess of everything.

The majority of us, it seems to me, will struggle with money in our twenties, and in order to get better at managing it we have to address the fact that we blame ourselves for it.

Our money-managing mantra is usually "it's all my fault". I've lost count of the times I've heard people claiming that women are just "bad" with cash, and I've said it myself. Money is so problematic that sometimes it's easier to get on board with the sexism that says you're stupid instead of admitting the scary truth—that even smart people struggle. We need to believe that we're good. We are smart, we are savvy, and we need to believe in ourselves if we're going to put ourselves in charge of our cash. We can't escape its influence, so we must escape the voice we carry around with us that claims we can't be in control of it, and we're not capable.

I bet you are already really good with money. If you plan your grocery shopping, or let your hair grow out to a weird angle because you're waiting for a Groupon for your favorite salon, or bring your own lunch into work, you're already killing it. But I think that it's important to talk about managing money in a way that isn't just screaming "SPEND AS LITTLE AS POSSIBLE!" I don't think people save up for cars and houses by buying all their toilet paper from the discount store. It's like the old cliché about loving yourself before you can be loved by others. If you want a bank balance that's worth being happy with, you need to see the worth in yourself.

Let's start, not with interest rates or tracker accounts or interest-free mortgages, but with treats. When we talk about money, we don't speak about the fact that it's necessary to factor in the odd splurge, and that if we budget for fun and frivolity, we're less likely to feel miserable when we hear the word "budget".

Again, I think this is where money talk gets sexist. We think of men "investing" in watches and cars, but women go on shopping "sprees". I have yet to hear two men urging each other, "Go on, be naughty! Get the three-liter engine, you're worth it!" But if we want to buy lipstick and dresses, we're told that they're silly and lack substance, which makes us feel as though we're silly, too.

When we do, inevitably, buy the stuff we like, it's really hard to think, "Good decision! This makes me very happy. I used my money in a wise way and now, every time I wear this dress, I shall feel pulled together, confident in my own autonomy and scorchingly hot! Hooray!" Our internal monologue is, more often than not, "Gosh, I do like this dress. Still, thirty pounds. That could have gone towards some bills. Or to charity. Mother Teresa would not have bought this dress. I'm a bad person. And it shows my tits, and that's not very Mother Teresa, either. Why am I showing my tits anyway? Am I sexy and confident in my body, or just an idiot tool of the patriarchy? Also, if I accidentally lean at a 45-degree angle, they actually look like a pair of voles trying to sneak into a badger den. FUCK! I should have just BURNED THIRTY POUNDS!"

Then we feel so miserable and uncertain about our financial acumen that we punish ourselves by buying nothing for six months, using toothpaste that costs twenty pence and getting a weekend job at a farm for the free milk, until we break in the face of our own austerity measures, get very drunk and spend £200 on eBay buying limited-edition commemorative mugs from the royal wedding.

In order to break this cycle of doom, I think that we all need a monthly allowance of fun bucks. Even if we can afford to invest just a single-figure sum in our own frivolity, we all need to know we can buy one thing on the spur of the moment just because we want it, and we don't have to justify it to anyone. If you always get to the end of the month and find that you're over your overdraft, and you always rush to Topshop on the first day and spend fifty pounds on foam sandals and feather earrings, some people would advise you to stay away from the shops. However, if spending cash on stuff with a limited shelf life truly makes you happy, I say that it's better to accept it as part of who you are, and see if you can find some extra pounds by switching to a cheaper phone package, or walking to work.

Obviously, there's nothing good or noble about piling up stuff for its own sake, and most of us already consume much more than we need, so a big part of managing money is learning to recognize and manage our appetites. When we shop, we need to buy the things that sate some part of ourselves. It doesn't matter if the longing is remote or hard to locate, if we feel a twinge of something somewhere, I don't think we have anything to gain by denying ourselves and losing out.

However, if we're just caught up in the lust to accumulate and we can hear our future selves muttering, "Why did you buy the inflatable Elvis bath cushion when you live in an apartment that only has a shower?" it's always best to listen to that voice and go home empty handed, but full of the confidence that comes with making a good decision. When we indulge our desires, we can control them—and when we deny ourselves for too long, I think they start to control us. So, if you're trying to develop a better relationship with money, I think the first thing to do is to set aside some cash for treats—even if it's less than five pounds a month, it will give you a sense of control, and you'll spend it on something you truly enjoy instead of perpetuating the starve/binge cycle that sends you on a frustrated splurge.

Most financial experts say that there's no point saving until you've cleared your debts, because the interest earned on savings is inevitably lower than the interest charged on borrowed money. I wish I'd ignored that advice and set up a small savings account as soon as I started to earn anything. A range of online savings accounts let you start with just £1, and if I'd put a tiny amount aside each month, I'd have felt less scared and better prepared. The thing about financial plans is that they're often derailed by unexpected events, such as a last-minute train journey or a broken item that needs repairing, and even a small cushion is a big help when it comes to managing your response and dealing with surprises. I think that having any sort of savings account makes us feel grown-up, strong, and in charge, no matter how little is in there.

When I ask around, most people tell me the hardest part of managing money is about managing other people's expectations, and dealing with friendships that are affected by everyone having different incomes and attitudes about how and where to spend their cash.

My friend Ari says:

Bill splitting has never stopped being painful. I've been the broke person picking at a salad, who has ended up paying for other people's steaks. I've started to deal with it by going out for dinner only when I'm flush, and ordering what I like—it means I don't ruin the experience by worrying throughout the meal. It was when a friend confided that she was worried about her credit card that I realized there is absolutely no shame in saying, "Sorry, I'm a bit strapped at the moment. Can we do it next month instead?"

I've had serious holiday FOMO when everyone else has gone on a fabulous trip, and I've spent months paying off a trip to Ibiza that I couldn't afford—in fact, I'm still paying it off, and for me, the anxiety that causes just wasn't worth the week of fun. At the moment, some friends are planning to go to New York, and I don't have the cash. I feel a bit sad about missing out, but I've started putting a bit of money aside when I can,

because I'd love to go one day—and when I do, I won't have
anything to worry about. I'm also thinking about saving for
some tiny Tiffany silver studs, and getting one of my friends to
buy them for me when they're there so that I have a fabulous
souvenir, even though I couldn't go on the trip!

Ultimately, achieving control of our cash is about giving ourselves more power and choice. It's easy to dismiss money matters because they seem bad, boring, or desperately daunting, but when we challenge and confront our financial fears, we feel confident and in control of so many other areas of our lives.

It's not about swimming in a vault filled with fifties, or aspiring to wear so many diamonds that you sink your own yacht. It's aiming to reach a point where you can buy yourself some time and quit the job you hate before rushing into another one, or you can break up with your boyfriend or girlfriend and move out of their apartment.

Remember, money is the last big taboo. For a long time, I thought I was alone in my struggle, but almost all of us will find it really hard at times. If you take a deep breath and talk about it, you'll probably feel better, and be amazed by the number of people you know who have scary stories to share. It takes a long time to build a safety net, but the sooner we're honest with ourselves about money, the faster we'll learn to use our tools.

DAISY DOES THIS!

➤ It's an obvious trick, but I have a standing order set up to put money into a savings account on the same day as my rent. If I'm going to spend a big chunk of money in one day, I might as well have a slightly larger amount going out, and I'm less likely to miss it.

➤ I did this totally by accident, but I have a good credit score because I've had credit cards in the past, and I've kept the cards I've paid off, so I have a large amount of credit "available" to me. As well as being helpful for trips abroad and absolute emergencies, I understand this score booster will be useful if I ever manage to buy a house. If I didn't have the cards and wanted to build up my credit score, I'd apply for one with a tiny limit and use it to pay for something small and regular, like a Netflix subscription—and pay it off at the end of every month.

➤ I try to remember that every time I have lusted after something wildly expensive and bought the cheaper version, I have usually ended up buying the pricey one in the end, too. If I want to save money, I try to economize on the stuff I really don't care about instead. On that subject, if you know anyone who has a thing for knock-off Céline sunglasses, please do send her in my direction. I have lots to get rid of.

➤ I try to be mindful of my emotions when it comes to money. The fact we have to manage it is an unavoidable part of life, and sometimes it has to be spent. I try to remember that if I've worked hard to earn it, I'm allowed to enjoy it, as long as I don't let it control me.

CHAPTER FIFTEEN

How To Make Mistakes

It's a warm June afternoon and, at twenty-five, I am embarking upon the defining moment of my career. I have never looked better, or felt cooler. In the air-conditioned splendor of BA's Heathrow business lounge, I'm sipping a chilly white wine with a laptop bag balanced on my knee, just like a legitimate, successful person. The businessmen—and sadly, it is mainly men—have not leaped up and shouted, "IMPOSTER! We know your sundress was £10 from Forever 21 and you're wearing a belt for a twelve-year-old that you've borrowed from a teen mag's fashion cupboard! We take business-class flights all the time, and it's obvious that this is your first, and probably only, and that it costs more than you earn in a month!" Sure, my sandals are looking a little greige after a long and sticky subway journey. Admittedly, the poshest part of my outfit, the white plastic Prada sunglasses, which I love like a firstborn, were paid for by secretly eBaying the phone headset that my mum bought me because she was frightened that I would get brain radiation. But I am on my way, figuratively and literally! I'm the sort of girl who gets sent to the South of France to meet movie stars! Not the sort who has one, unflattering bikini, which she only ever wears under her clothes when she (regularly) runs out of clean underwear.

I am professional and successful, so I want to allow plenty of time to get to my gate. I'm a swan. I glide past Gucci, pretending their new tote bags don't interest me, when I'd probably live on the street for weeks to get my hands on one (and I'd have to). I even avoid the mini drugstores, resisting the temptation to buy £50-worth of tiny shampoos and hand sanitizers. I get to the gate. First one there. I feel smug, then strange, then after twenty minutes, slightly scared. It's weird that no one is here—and that the screen says "Zurich" when I'm going to Nice.

Fuck.

After checking a board and looking for reassurance, I realize that I have to be at the other end of the terminal and the gate shuts in seven minutes. So, I run. My strides are as wide as baby elephants, and I can't work out whether I'm crying or if my face is wet with sweat. I am a disaster. I'm the worst journalist in the world—the worst person in the world. Anyone else would be able to get this right. I'm going to get fired, and I deserve it. To think that I spent the last hour believing I belonged in this world. I'm mentally beating myself up while running, and suddenly my right foot lands on the back of my left flip-flop and I'm horizontal, laptop falling out of my bag, flying over my head and landing with a thump, while my sunglasses spin through the air.

I make it to the gate, weeping and apologizing, and kindly stewards lead me to the pre-flight pen for tiny children, the elderly, and the infirm. On boarding, the man with the seat next to mine mutters something to his friend behind him about the "sexy girl"—then sees my face, which now has the color and consistency of a tin of chopped tomatoes. He switches seats.

Eventually, I made it to Monte Carlo, filed my piece, and kept my job. If the worst imaginable thing happened and I'd missed my plane, I could have got another one. Nice isn't that far away. Even if I had been fired, I wouldn't have died. At some point, I would have found another job. Ultimately, this mistake didn't teach me anything about business trips, or airports, or that you should shout, "I DON'T BELIEVE YOU!" when the person at the check-in desk gives you a gate number. But I learned about perspective, and catastrophic thinking. A mistake, by definition, is an error. You don't make mistakes on purpose, but as humans we have to live in a world with infinite variables, and hundreds and thousands and millions of things to worry about. My first mistake—not double-checking my gate number because I was too busy being excited about the free tiny toothbrushes in the lounge washroom—was a tiny one. The bigger, more worrying error was failing to deal with the consequences calmly, and running across the airport and away from my better judgment like it was on fire.

Most of the time, I'm smart enough to make good choices. I don't count my chickens before they're hatched, and I make sure to cook them properly. I won't go out without a coat. I set multiple alarms "just in case", I write appointments in diaries and I meet my deadlines. Periodically, I'll miss something, or get caught in a moment and do something thoughtless. We're constantly thinking and can become angry and abusive towards ourselves if we stop, or make an imperfect decision. But I believe logic is a finite resource, and at least one time out of a hundred, it will fail us. That doesn't mean we've failed. Imagine a computer running several separate internet browsers, each with several windows and hundreds of open tabs. It's going to get incredibly slow, and then it's going to crash. That's the brain. We overload it, and when something goes wrong, we're really mean to ourselves about it.

We forget that making mistakes is actually positive—they're essential if we want to learn and progress. I wasted so much of my twenties hating myself for not being perfect and not knowing everything straight away, but I was working out how to be. At twenty-five, thirty-five, and even older, we're all relatively new adults. Although we're discovering new situations and understanding how the world works, learning from your mistakes is less important than learning how to have a perspective on them. If we're so frightened of failing that we avoid every area in which we might get something wrong, we'll never grow up into the people we deserve to become.

Throughout my twenties I spent a lot of time looking for a "cheat sheet" that might help me to avoid what I thought were all the typical mistakes, including being in the wrong relationship, not doing well at work, having no money, living in the wrong place, and being unhappy. Yet I managed to make mistakes in every single one of these areas—probably more than I would have done if I hadn't been so focused on not failing. I dreamed about being a journalist, but thought that I wasn't the sort of person who got to achieve her dreams and so I was better off doing a sensible, practical job where I might not face rejection. Then I got fired, and pursued what I really wanted when I had nothing left to lose. I stayed in bad relationships because I thought things would get better if I stopped making mistakes, when the only mistake was staying and failing to see that I wasn't the problem. I thought that I was constantly and horribly broke because I was making money-management mistakes. Admittedly, this part was, and is, slightly true, but I wasted a lot of time being ashamed of myself when I really should have embraced the fact that I was doing the best I could with what I had.

Growing up isn't about getting to a point where you no longer make mistakes—learning to survive them is what helps you to mature. Very few of us are haunted by the real consequences of our errors. I shudder with shame to remember the way some mistakes made me feel at the time, from accidentally closing doors on people when I didn't realize they were behind me to calling my old (male) math teacher "Mum", but genuinely life-altering mistakes are rare. However, they do happen.

I've set kitchens on fire by leaving tea towels on top of hot electric hobs. I've slept with strange men and woken up stranded with nothing but a Google map and an iPhone with a 3 percent battery left to guide me home. I've burned off my own bangs while blowing out birthday candles. I've gone to a festival and spent a whole month's rent in two days on cider and falafel. But, my worst mistake needlessly caused hurt and distress to a whole group of people.

One of the less attractive parts of my character is that I adore gossip, or to give it the correct name, bitching. Once, when I was drunk at a party and trying to impress a person I did not know well, I thought it would be clever to give her the inside track on some mutual friends who were sleeping together—one of them had a girlfriend, who didn't know about it.

My new acquaintance was appalled, and shortly afterwards told the girlfriend and confronted the hook-up friends, naming me as the source. Now, four people were furious with me—the girlfriend, for my lack of loyalty, my main friends, for telling on them and sharing a secret that wasn't really mine to give away, and the new person, because she correctly surmised that giving her this information was unfair to everyone, put her in a position she didn't want to be in and was actually a really shitty thing to do.

It was a shock. It wasn't the first time I'd done something similarly stupid, but it was the first time I'd been called out, as well as being the only occasion when I couldn't immediately fix what I'd broken. Saying "sorry" wasn't going to take anyone's pain away or make them feel any less angry with me—even though I really meant it.

Eventually, I managed to rebuild a friendship with one of my old friends, although it's still a bit strained. She doesn't confide in me anymore, and I don't blame her. My other friend and his (ex)girlfriend don't speak to me. I betrayed them both in different ways. It happened almost ten years ago but thinking of all the pain I created turns my blood to acid. I'll never stop feeling ashamed, and I'm not sure that I deserve to.

Ultimately, you don't know how you'll behave in any situation until you're immersed in it. Maybe the friends who were having the affair also felt as though they'd made a mistake, but that's not my call to make. Personally, I don't think it's advisable to begin a relationship with someone behind existing partners' backs, but there are all sorts of reasons and mitigating circumstances that might lead you there. However, I can't think of anything that justifies sharing cruel gossip. I wish I could—I'd sleep easier!

However, the horrible experience taught me an incredibly important lesson—careless talk costs lives. Some actions have much bigger consequences than losing a job or missing a plane. I'd chosen not to talk to my cheating friends about what I knew, which meant I'd forfeited the right to talk about it ever. The only true, life-altering mistakes are failures of kindness.

Often, the consequence of a mistake is that I fail to be kind to myself, but in this instance I knew I'd done something wrong in not respecting other people. I've subsequently stopped myself from making similar mistakes by asking myself, "Is this nice? Could this hurt someone who isn't me?"

It's all well and good being curdled with shame, and deciding that your mistake is so dreadful that it would be easier, more comfortable if you threw yourself down a well, but to be a proper grown-up, you have to make the mistake count.

I think one of the strangest things about growing up is the discovery that you don't automatically get found out for every single mistake you make—and weirdly, this often makes things worse. When I feel as though I've got away with something, I become less circumspect and more slapdash. At university, I slid from being a smart student to a lazy coaster when I accidentally read the wrong book one week. No one seemed to mind, and I found it pretty easy to take part in a discussion on a text that I knew nothing about. My first mistake didn't seem to have any immediate consequences, so I started to care less, and get sloppier. The mistakes piled up, and compounded, and I found myself getting left behind.

Eventually, I had to admit that it was down to me to identify and fix the problem. My punishment wasn't being told off—it was having to live with the consequences of what I'd done, or in my case hadn't done. I'd been drinking off-brand wine coolers in the park when I should have been in the library.

I paid for my mistakes with worry. I thought the consequences of my bad decisions would lead to me leaving university with no degree, and struggling to get a job to pay off the mountains of debt that I'd amassed. On dark days, I wondered whether my first mistake had been applying for the course in the first place, and if I should have just stayed with my parents and carried on working as a checkout supervisor, where my biggest challenge had involved cleaning up after a three-year-old who had just vomited over a display of live gourmet cress.

As I've already mentioned, I ended up, shockingly, getting a degree I was quite pleased with, even though it wasn't the result of three years' hard work, but three weeks of frantic cramming. However, it's not had any demonstrable impact on my life. No one cares. What is significant is that I spent most of the year after graduation feeling miserable and inadequate after accepting a job offer that I didn't really want, because I was so worried about my results that I did ridiculous things as I attempted to shore up the future that I thought I'd ruined for myself. Have you ever burned a hole in a carpet, thought about telling the landlord and decided instead to take a twenty-five- mile bus journey to buy a £10 rug from Ikea so that you can hide the burn and forget about it until your tenancy ends and your landlord wants to keep £800 of your deposit for a new carpet? Mistakes borne of optimism aren't hard to fix. It's the mistakes you make when you fail to have faith in yourself, the ones that happen when you're scared and sneaky, that are the hardest to recover from. More cheerfully, they're the ones that have the most to teach us. So, what did I learn?

Looking back, my time at university taught me about misplaced pride. I could have saved myself so much heartache and terror if I'd been strong enough to put my hand up sometimes and say, "I don't understand." I thought the short-term shame in getting something wrong was bigger than the long-term issue of feeling stupid and keeping it secret. If I'd spoken out and said that I felt out of my depth at the beginning, I might have been given the help I needed and felt much more confident towards the end of my studies and got something really worthwhile out of the academic experience.

I thought that success was all about looking and seeming impressive, and that way of thinking led me away from learning and straight to a job that made me deeply unhappy.

I also learned that it's usually hard work that makes something worth having. Before I started higher education, I was lucky enough to find most parts of school fairly easy. If I was good at it, I did well at it, and if I wasn't, I just didn't bother and said I wasn't interested. As a university student,

I learned that having a natural aptitude for something wasn't going to give me the edge, and found myself in an environment where hard work, not winging it, was recognized and rewarded. When I started my course, I thought that if I didn't know it all already, I didn't want to know—but in some ways, the goal should have been to feel stupider than I did when I arrived, having learned the world was far bigger than I imagined.

Years later, in a yoga class, I heard the instructor explaining that it was far better for your body to do part of the posture properly than it was to do a flawed, flukily perfect-looking Tree Pose that you'd thrown together using a combination of hypermobility and sweat, having perspired so hard that you'd managed to glue your palm organically to your ankle. There is no shame in making a mistake when you genuinely believe in what you're doing, but when you know you're faking it, and you start to spin out of control because you're too frightened to admit you're lost and need help, your mistakes will wear you down. You'll end up damaging your joints if you're in a yoga class, and if you're in any other situation, you'll start to destroy your fundamental understanding of who you are.

Now I realize that life is much richer if you can relish not knowing, cherish the chance to come to something anew, and challenge your own ignorance. The three scariest, most significant words in the English language aren't "I love you"—they're "I don't know". Saying that takes guts, but as soon as you can manage it, you're ready to start making some seriously brilliant mistakes, the ones that crop up because you have hope and faith in yourself, and you truly believe you might be capable of anything—and you'll have a go.

So, how do you get past the difficult, damaging mishaps and start making great mistakes, or, if you prefer, Blunders of Wonder? I think that the first, and hardest, lesson to get our heads around is that most great triumphs and achievements are a result of a series of tiny mistakes. You might start with nothing more than an idea, a vague sense of hope and the assumption that you might be able to eBay your Limited Edition Beanie Babies if something goes seriously wrong. It does. You could come to the conclusion that it was a mistake to plan to quit your job and travel the seven seas on an inflatable sofa, or start a business making artisanal jewelry out of paperclips, and give up; or you could analyze your mistakes, work out what went wrong and keep refining your idea until you're ready to have another go. Mistakes are difficult to recover from because they damage our pride but if we can get some distance from them, work out how to interpret them in a useful way, and then take a deep breath and try again, understanding we'll make even more mistakes, we'll soon have an entire collection of platinum stationery, or an ocean-going three-piece suite.

In the past, when I've made a mistake, from getting someone's name wrong to misreading a map and giving dodgy directions, I haven't worried about the consequences and how they'll affect me as much as I've feared other people's reactions. Will they be angry? Will they think I'm stupid? Will I spend the rest of my life running out of rooms as people shout, "Not this idiot! She said *Game of Thrones* in the pub quiz when she meant *The Hunger Games*! We hate her!" But when other people make mistakes, I do my very best to be compassionate and understanding. When we talk about human error, we need to remember the human bit, and the fact that we are who we are because we occasionally make a misguided or impulsive choice, and then make a mess of things. When we make mistakes, we make progress, and we only struggle to recover from them when we can't be kind.

If we can get better at forgiving ourselves, we'll become braver, and we'll also be more compassionate and encouraging when the people in our lives get it wrong. I asked a few friends to talk about the biggest mistake of their twenties, and every single one had a thoughtful answer. At no point did I think, "I can't believe you did that, you fool!" They had all learned about themselves as a result of the mistake, and made positive decisions as a result of their discoveries.

Marisa, who is thirty:

I spent a long time wondering if breaking up with my long-term boyfriend was a mistake. We'd been living together, and giving up my partner and my home at twenty-six felt like setting light to my life. It took me a while to find out who I was without him, but all the crazy, life-altering, wonderful, soul-shaping things I've done without him have been the proof it wasn't the mistake I thought it was.

Jess, who is twenty-eight:

I've gone for jobs I didn't get, stayed friends with people who were toxic, and dated people I should never have gone out with, but realistically I wouldn't be so happy now if I hadn't made the mistakes that taught me to appreciate what I have.

Lauren, who is twenty-seven:

My mistake is not letting myself make more mistakes—the boys I was too coy with, the fights I never picked, the invites I turned down and the opportunities I never took because I was too cautious and worried about getting it wrong. And going on the gameshow The Weakest Link *and getting the wrong answer to 36 minus 29. That was pretty bad.*

The words of these women prove that the old cliché is true—we mostly regret what we *didn't* do. Even if something becomes difficult to endure, we'd rather look back and feel as though we did our best to do the right thing than say that we stood on the sidelines because we were frightened. You can be the sort of person who gets a question wrong on *The Weakest Link* or the one who would love to have a go but decides the risk of failure is too daunting and stays at home instead. No one wants to fail, but when we focus on it, we let fear control our decisions. If nothing else, making mistakes usually proves that the consequences are never as bad as we imagine. Learning to embrace our mistakes increases the faith we have in ourselves, and the stronger that grows, the better our decisions get.

DAISY DOES THIS!

➤ Now I know that the biggest mistake I can make is not trying something because I'm scared of getting it wrong, I'm much braver. I have accepted that mistakes are inevitable, and life is more exciting.

➤ If I've made a mistake, I tell someone straight away, because feeling humiliated and being helped when the mistake is manageable is much better than covering it up and being found out when the server crashes/housemates get evicted/the hole in the wall becomes so big that a fox gets through it and you find it on the sofa watching *Pointless*.

➤ I remember I'm not alone. When a mistake feels big and bad, it's easy for me to feel lost, and worry that no one else has ever got it wrong before. So, I think about how even Rachel Maddow has probably been late renewing her car insurance or forgotten her mum's birthday.

➤ Over time, I've learned that a mistake is seriously awful only when I panic over it, and make lots of tiny, breathless, thoughtless mistakes in an attempt to fix it. It's usually better if I sleep on it, or at least sit down with a cup of tea and a cookie while it sinks in.

CHAPTER SIXTEEN

How To Have A Happy Beginning

Enough is enough, I told myself after limping home from the hospital ER, following a date in which I had ended up falling off Nelson's Column.

I'd gathered plenty of stories, but I wasn't having fun. Dating didn't make me feel good. I needed to work out how to be enough on my own. I still hoped for the Big Love, but I knew that unless I worked out how to stop looking and love my own company, I wasn't searching properly—I was just treading water.

In my hunt for storybook romance, I'd complained that men didn't buy flowers anymore, or take you out for fancy dinners. Well, what good was feminism if I couldn't do it myself? I filled my room with stargazer lilies and candles, and served myself rare rib eye. It was like eating steak in church. I spent whole days by myself, striding about the city, learning about where I lived and how the roads joined up. I found a quiet, calm strength in being on my own. On the day of my twenty-seventh birthday, I vowed that it was going to be the year when I learned to love myself a little bit better. I'd spent most of my twenties searching for the sensation, but it would only ever come to me if it came from me first.

I met my husband the very next day.

In the spirit of full disclosure, it wasn't love at first sight. It was a series of dates that were awkward enough to make me suspicious and compelling enough to make me stick around.

He was everything I ever dreamed of—and I was bewildered by it. "He's generous, imaginative, creative. He does everything he says that he'll do. He tells me how he feels about me, he likes spending time with me. This is very confusing," I complained to friends. There had been no turning up to dates late and drunk, no penis pictures, no forgotten wallets. This was not twenty-first-century dating as I knew it. What could he be up to? I came very close to sacking it off, masochistically, for someone who canceled every other date, made me cry once a week, and thought my name was "Maisie". But even my subconscious knew I was being foolish, and my mates agreed with it. "I really like the sound of this man," said my friend Zoe. "It's about bloody time that you went out with someone who's nice to you." Instead of dating the people who made me work to be worthy of them, it was time to make a go of it with someone who wanted to prove that they were worthy of me.

I'm so glad that I was so bad at dating for most of my twenties. I was—am—an idiot. I had to learn the same obvious lessons, by rote, over and over, but they've finally stuck. My worst boyfriends made me feel as though I needed them, that I was nothing without them, that they completed me somehow. My husband makes me feel that I'm strong enough on my own. Of course, I'm my very best self when I'm with him, but every day, I want him more than I need him.

He taught me that love is patient, love is kind, love is calm and quiet. It's not a music video of big hair, big tears, and erotic, electrical storms. It's two people pottering about a small flat making each other coffee. It's waking up every morning and feeling quietly delighted as you smell the sleep on his skin and observe the way his tufty hair is framed by the pillow. It's sly hands sneaking up jumpers to stroke the silky skin underneath, and wanting to share all your big news, bad news, and pictures of especially adorable dogs. It's knowing that there's nothing that can't be talked over and solved by a walk to the park or a trip to the pub.

In some ways, I could feel pretty smug and sorted about how I've got through my twenties and met a love "target". I'm married to the man I love. I wear a shiny ring on my left hand. Distant relatives have bought us a whole department store-worth of overpriced plates. This has to be my happy ending, surely?

Well, I'm hoping for a happy beginning. I know less about love at thirty-one than I thought I knew at twenty, but I have learned that we can't protect ourselves from our own mistakes, although those mistakes are rarely made in vain. It's nice if your Big Love is handsome, or clever, or funny—but all that really matters is that he's kind to you, and supports you when you're kind to yourself. We can't future-proof love. When we're with someone, we're vulnerable. Love is dangerous, and there's no way of doing it safely. There is no condom for the heart.

But we can protect ourselves with self-love, and the knowledge that we don't need anyone to complete us. We can't be with anyone who makes us feel as though we're not enough on our own.

I don't think I needed a man to fix me, but I needed to fix myself before I was ready to meet anyone. If you look to someone else to make you whole, it will break you. Meeting and marrying the love of your life by the time you're thirty is not a helpful goal to have. It's much better to get your emotional house in order first. Even if you have to wait another ten, twenty or fifty years, you'll be ready to build, grow, and make love last.

That's been the greatest growing-up lesson I have learned over the last few years: I am able to build something that will stay up. And if it does fall down, I'll know what to do. I am capable of so much more than I realized. Every triumph and disaster has taught me that I'm surprisingly strong. I can rush to future-proof problems, to anticipate potential disasters and visualize every way in which they can break me. However, that hasn't always worked, and it's often meant that I've missed the best moments of my own life because I'm waiting for something to go wrong. I had thought growing up was about trying to stay five steps ahead of my problems, but now I think it's about learning to stay still and be present sometimes. We can't stop bad things from happening, and we can't make good things last forever. However, we can accept our perfectly imperfect selves with compassion and kindness. These are the qualities that make the best grown-ups.

How To Grow Up

What I've Learned Over The Last Decade (And What I'd Tell My Twenty-Year-Old Self)

ALWAYS be prepared to say, "I'm sorry." NEVER follow it up with "but".

Salad is delicious. Burgers are delicious. The "good" food is the one you actually fancy eating at the time. The "bad" food is the one you take eight pictures of in order to delay the awful moment when you actually have to put it in your mouth.

Never date someone who wouldn't, in an emergency, lend you their toothbrush.

Doctors, bank managers, and bosses might seem scary, but they generally want good things for you and they're going to help before they tell you off. After the age of twenty-two, the only person who can really still tell you off is your mother.

If you feel as though the world is ending, the apocalypse can be postponed by singing Beyoncé songs in the shower.

It doesn't matter whether someone is rich, clever, funny, fluent in seventeen languages, able to make their own butter, or has a billion trillion Instagram followers unless they are, first and foremost, very kind.

Don't ever be too scared to reply to a question with, "I don't know."

Almost everything will eventually seem hilarious.

If you don't want to ask the person you're seeing if you're "official" because you're worried about scaring them off, stop seeing that person! You want someone who's more "member of your fan club" and less "snooty doorman who won't let you in the club".

Sometimes eating dinner at a table, with proper cutlery, can fix the thing that drove you to eat your last meal straight from the fridge with a spoon.

On that theme, don't sit on the sofa to eat soup.

Remember that you will rarely want or use the second and third items in a three-for-two offer.

If you can, avoid working for anyone who wouldn't be kind if they caught you crying in parking lot.

When someone sees you naked for the first time, they should react as though you're Oprah and you've just shouted, "You get a car!" If they fail to display this level of enthusiasm, order an Uber and make sure one of you gets in it and leaves.

If at all possible, try to live somewhere that has a bathtub that can be wallowed in for a solid hour.

It is quite normal to feel tearful and irrational by day five of a holiday. It doesn't mean that you hate your friends and need to move to a silent Buddhist temple.

To avoid bad, vomity hangovers, remember this simple rhyme when ordering cocktails: if it's blue, it's not for you.

The only person who really needs to like your selfie is YOU.

If you can light a scented candle without burning your house down, you are a successful adult.

Thanks And Acknowledgements

This book was brought into being because I've been incredibly lucky and had the chance to work with a number of talented, dedicated people. Firstly, my agent, Diana Beaumont, who is always indefatigable, intelligent and kind—and inspires me to push myself and do my best instead of giving up and retiring to my bed to eat Kettle Chips. Also, her assistant and early reader Aneesa Mirza, whose warmth and generosity kept me writing and stopped me from throwing my laptop out of the window.

Also, enormous thanks to the team at Headline, past and present. Rachel Kenny, Emma Tait, Sarah Emsley, Georgina Moore, Phoebe Swinburn, Vicky Palmer, Helena Fouracre—I could not love you more. You are so wonderful to work with, and your wisdom, compassion, and infectious energy has made this joyous.

It wouldn't have been possible without kind, helpful friends, many of whom generously shared stories with me, and supported me so much when I first started to wonder whether this could ever exist in book form. Amy, Ana, Caroline, Cathy, Claire, Corinne, Emma G., Gail, Helen L., Helen N., Heloise, Holly, Janina, Jess, Jude, Kat, Katy, Laura J.W., Lizzie B., Lizzie W., Lynn, Marian, Marie-Claire, Marina, Rebecca, Marisa, Nina P, Nina S., Poppy, Roshni, Sarah D, Sarah P., Jo, Sam, Scarlett—this is an inadequate way of saying that I am permanently indebted to you, and I owe you a handwritten note of thanks and an enormous drink. Also, love and thanks to all the kind people who keep me company all day long on Twitter.

Special love and thanks to Lauren, Dolly, and Angela, kind, wise, early readers who gave me invaluable advice, and countless patient responses to needy, frantic all-caps WhatsApp messages.

Much love to my old *Bliss* friends and bosses—Angeli, Zoe, Leslie, Fatima, Nadine, Frankie, Lisa, Charlotte, Charlie, Katie, Lydia—working with you all was the best job in the world, and inspired so much of this book.

My amazing sisters—this is for you with all my love, and I'm sorry-not-sorry that I keep stealing your stories (I'll stop when you stop being funnier than me). Mum and Dad, best parents in the world, thank you for everything from sharing your love of writers and writing, to loving and looking after me when I've been struggling with the grown-up world. (Also, please don't read pages 152–73. Thank you.)

This is also for my husband, the love of my life, my very best friend, and my happy beginning. You are the finest grown-up I know.